PURCHASING
FOR CHEFS
A Concise Guide

ANDREW HALE FEINSTEIN
JOHN M. STEFANELLI

WILEY
JOHN WILEY & SONS, INC.

Copyright © 2007 by John Wiley & Sons, Inc. All rights reserved

Published by John Wiley & Sons, Inc., Hoboken, New Jersey
Published simultaneously in Canada

For general information on our other products and services or for technical
support, please contact our Customer Care Department within the United States
at (800) 762-2974, outside the United States at (317) 572-3993 or fax (317) 572-4002.

Wiley also publishes its books in a variety of electronic formats. Some content that
appears in print may not be available in electronic books. For more information
about Wiley products, visit our web site at www.wiley.com.

Library of Congress Cataloging-in Publication Data:
Feinstein, Andrew Hale.
Purchasing for chefs : a concise guide / Andrew Hale Feinstein, John M. Stefanelli.
   p. cm.
Includes index.
ISBN-13: 978-0-471-72898-6 (pbk.)
ISBN-10: 0-471-72898-5 (pbk.)
1. Hospitality industry—Purchasing. I. Stefanelli, John M. II. Title.
TX911.3.P8F455   2007
647.95068'7—dc22

                                                              2005035003

Printed in the United States of America

10 9 8 7 6 5 4 3 2

CONTENTS

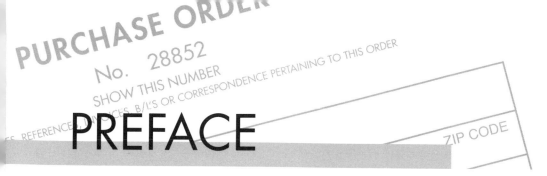

PREFACE

You might be wondering what a couple of ivory tower academics can tell you about purchasing. We bring a unique combination of experiences and education to this book. Between us we have more than 60 years of restaurant/hospitality experience, both in the trenches as well as in the classrooms and laboratories of major universities. We have written several books, articles, and newspaper/magazine stories, given many speeches, and conducted many seminars/workshops. We've both worked for years in several types of foodservice operations before entering the world of education. And John supervised the William F. Harrah College of Hotel Administration's restaurant and catering facilities for about 12 years, with Andy taking on that role about two years ago. We think we know what it takes to administer a cost-effective purchasing and inventory management system in this industry. In this book, we show you how to do it.

"So what?" you say. "I need something that will work. Something for a person like me who doesn't have all day to think about it, talk about it, or write about it. I have to *do* it."

Well, you've come to the right place.

Like many projects, this one began with a "what if" question. The folks at Wiley instigated it. Someone there asked us what we thought of taking our massive university purchasing text (approximately 700 pages) and condensing it to the point where a culinary student could learn the basics of purchasing in a three-week course or a chef could read it in one sitting and immediately put it to work. The book you now hold is the outcome of that initial conversation. It contains only the essentials of purchasing, easily read on most plane rides.

This book is unique. It is not comparable to the typical purchasing books you see on amazon.com. It contains precise, specific information unencumbered by a ton of theory and speculation. You want to know how much to buy, you got it. You want to know how to manage product so that belt-tightening doesn't choke the employees while simultaneously making the owners happy, you got that, too. And if you want to know how to keep pilferage at a level that satisfies employees, but allows you to meet your sales and cost targets, ditto. This book tells you what to do and how to do it. Although it's necessary for us to present options once in a while, this is primarily a left-foot, right-foot discussion. These are the basics, along with a few extras. Take what you want and leave the rest.

Having said that, we do need to remind you that there is not usually one right way or wrong way to do *anything* in the restaurant business. There are just different ways. We think we have the right combination and can help you improve your operation, but who knows? The information in this book has worked for us and many chefs in the business. We think it will work for you, too.

To help make these points clear, we've included the following features:

- ☑ Chapter outline
- ☑ Learning objectives
- ☑ Apply What You've Learned questions that present realistic situations that require you to analyze them
- ☑ Discussion questions
- ☑ "Purchasing Terminology," a short guide to purchasing lingo that goes beyond the scope of the book.

There is an Instructor's Manual (ISBN: 0-471-7898-3) available. Qualified instructors can also access the Instructor's Manual on the companion Web site www.wiley.com/college.

It took a lot of people a lot of time to put this package together. We had a great deal of help along the way, and we would like to thank everyone who contributed his or her time and energy. We especially want to thank the following colleagues: George Baggott, Jean Hertzman, and Reid A. Paul. We would also like to thank those who reviewed this book: Chef Peter T. Adams of The Illinois Institute of Art, Chef William Apicerno of Connecticut Culinary Institute, Greg Forte of Utah Valley State College, Chef John Laloganes of Cooking and Hospitality Institute of Chicago, Chef Ken Narcavage of Western Culinary Institute, Marie Porter Royce of California Polytechnic Institute, and Gary Schwartz of Asheville Buncombe Technological Community College.

But enough talk. Start thinking, start buying.

Andrew Hale Feinstein
John Stefanelli

PURCHASE ORDER

No. 28852

SHOW THIS NUMBER

SES, REFERENCES, INVOICES, B/L'S OR CORRESPONDENCE PERTAINING TO THIS ORDER

ZIP CODE

ZIP CODE

UNIT PRICE

DATE REQUIRED

DESCRIPTION

UNIT

1

MENU
PLANNING

What Kind of Stuff Should I Sell?

CHAPTER OUTLINE

- THINGS TO CONSIDER WHEN PLANNING THE MENU
- TYPES OF MENUS
- KNOW THY GUEST

LEARNING OBJECTIVES

☑ Identify what determines what a foodservice operation sells.

☑ Identify the categories of menu misrepresentation.

☑ Be familiar with the many types of menus that foodservice operations use.

☑ Design a menu that meets the needs of the operation, works within the operation's constraints, and contains no areas of misrepresentation.

☑ Develop menu items that address consumers' wants and needs.

Before you buy any foods or beverages you have to have a good handle on what you're planning to sell. This is likewise true for things you buy but don't resell, such as cleaning chemicals, paper products, outside service contractors, and so forth.

We learn very early in our careers that it all begins with the menu. We can't do anything until we have it in place. Let's take a few minutes to review some of the highlights of menu planning.

THINGS TO CONSIDER WHEN PLANNING THE MENU

There are tons of things that affect what you can sell and what your menu includes. You have to be careful when putting menus together. You have to ensure that you are selling something that you can produce and serve correctly and profitably. Consider the following when deciding what you should serve to your guests.

▪ RESTAURANT LAYOUT AND DESIGN

If you're planning a new restaurant, you usually have a great deal of flexibility. You can see to it that the restaurant location and construction are consistent with your desired menu. Unfortunately, you often need to work with existing facilities. Whereas the initial menu for a new property works well, the inevitable shifts in your customer base and in societal trends will demand that you continually revise the menu. Sooner or later you will bump into a situation where your current facilities can't support some menu changes. It brings to mind a local operation that wanted to add panini sandwiches, but after purchasing the necessary cooking equipment, found out that it wouldn't fit on the work table. Furthermore, additional electrical power had to be brought in, creating more construction cost than originally anticipated. Be careful here. Don't put something on the menu until you're reasonably sure that it will not cause insurmountable problems.

For beverage service in your restaurant, layout and design isn't likely to be very troublesome. The typical bar layout and design is pretty standardized and can accommodate most beverage menu changes. The only exception is if you try to institute a major beverage alcohol program, such as adding numerous draft beers, in a property that is not set up to allow such a drastic change.

▪ PRODUCT AVAILABILITY/CONSISTENCY

This is a serious issue if you plan a menu that you'll be using for some time. For instance, if you plan a menu that relies on quite a few fresh seasonal ingredients, you will pay a premium for a lower-quality product during the off-season. This is why many restaurants have menus that include a section of popular foods and beverages that doesn't change very much—products that can easily be obtained throughout the year. These menus also have a section of "specials" that change from day to day depending upon what's available. Seafood houses are a good example of this strategy.

▪ TYPE OF EQUIPMENT

The more elaborate and lengthy the menu, the more equipment you'll need. Furthermore, you may have to purchase sophisticated, expensive equipment. We like to buy equipment that can perform many duties. We also like the quick-disconnect items, which ensure a greater amount of flexibility, especially valuable if you do a lot of catering. But most of us in this business have to settle for what we have.

You also need to be very cautious when listening to equipment **sales reps** go on about how much you can do with their particular equipment product line. A lot of this is trade puffery; don't fall for it.

Do yourself a favor and learn how to cook on a campfire if necessary. Some day you will take on a new position where the menu is in place. You will have to live with it for quite a while. The good chefs can cook on anything if they have to. You have to be able to do that or you'll go nuts.

■ STORAGE

This is one of the most challenging things we face in our business. No one wants to pay top dollar to rent a building in a prime retail area so that part of it can be devoted to storing No. 10 cans. It's similar to the lack of proper equipment many chefs encounter as they practice their craft throughout their careers, only worse. Lack of storage will severely restrict what you can do. If you try to put out a menu that is too ambitious, storage deficiencies will force you to spend a lot of time seeking vendors who provide daily deliveries. This puts a tremendous strain on your operation—and your sanity. Sooner or later you'll reduce the menu offerings to fit your storage capabilities, a strategy that could backfire if your target market seeks more variety than you are able to produce.

■ LABOR

The number of work hours you are allowed to schedule, as well as the typical labor skill under your direction, will have an immense impact on your menu offerings. You won't have the luxury of dropping things from the menu because you don't have the right labor force. If they don't know how to do something, you will have to show them how to do it. Chefs have to be good teachers.

If you have a tight labor pool, and/or a tight labor budget, you can fudge a little and purchase convenience foods to compensate. But these are horribly expensive, and their purchase prices are not always offset by a lower labor cost.

Get used to having a tight labor budget. Keep in mind that labor includes the wages/salaries you pay, plus payroll taxes (like social security and workers' comp) and various other benefits that are up to you or your company's discretion (such as health insurance and 401(k) plans). In a Las Vegas Casino/Hotel, for every dollar paid to a culinary union employee, the property pays approximately $0.60 for payroll taxes and other benefits. Whoa!

Here's another interesting story. An accountant for a food and beverage management program at a school had her hours reduced, but her hourly wages increased substantially. She was making the same amount of money working less hours. However, she no longer received retirement or health insurance benefits. The savings worked out to approximately $3,000 per year for the program. At that time, the amount of annual sales revenue needed to generate a $3,000 profit was approximately $12,000. In this case, she didn't mind the change, since her other part-time accounting job gave her full benefits. Chefs, welcome to the world of labor management.

■ GUEST DESIRES

Can't forget the guest; he or she is the reason we come to work every day. You have to know as much as possible about your guests because their tastes are ever changing. One day they can't get enough of the low-carb diet; the next day they're calling for the pasta salad. It's difficult to stay on top of your target market because their tastes change little by little. Just when you think you have it down, you don't.

In the best of all worlds, you would be the one directing their tastes with new and exciting menu offerings. But even then you may have rules that can't be broken. John once worked a summer in a country club bakery where the pastry chef could be creative as long as he didn't run out of Boston cream pie.

Another thing to keep in mind about your customers is that a large portion of the customer base (baby boomers) is getting older each day. And each day their discretionary income changes, up or down. Their family situations change. Many are influenced by all of the food shows on TV and on the Internet. And you have to put up with customer churn—that is, some old ones leave you, some new ones come on board. We suppose this is why you see so many chefs these days working the dining rooms and designing exhibition kitchens, personally trying to stay up on the latest shifts in customer demands.

■ FOOD AND BEVERAGE TRENDS

A big part of understanding your market is trying to discern what's hot right now. Another challenge is to determine if something new is a trend versus a short-lived fad. The best way to do this is to read the things your typical guests read, watch the shows they watch, and so on. You have to think like them or you're not going to be able to satisfy their needs.

Furthermore, trends go beyond the products you serve. Other things, such as décor, atmospherics, take-out and delivery options, and hours of operation, will also have an effect on your business. A former food and beverage director at Caesars Palace once told one of our classes that the most frustrating thing he encountered in his career was the fact that every detail, no matter how seemingly insignificant, is critical in a food and beverage establishment.

A restaurant owner who never served a cup of coffee in his life before investing in a theme restaurant because he thought it would be fun, remarked that his most frustrating experience was finding that if you screwed up even one little thing, you could never make the guest happy. His primary business was in the bedding industry, and he noted the contrast: A customer buys a bed set and it's delivered the next day. If it's scratched, no problem. The driver gets back on the truck, takes down another one, puts it in your home, it's perfect. Most of the time, you're happy. But if you get a lousy appetizer, you won't be happy the rest of the meal. And worst of all, you'll blab about your bad experience to anyone who will listen. And they wonder why we restaurant folks are a little "off-center."

■ TRUTH IN MENU

Be careful about what you say on your menu. You don't want to mislead people. In some parts of the country there are laws prohibiting menu misrepresentation. But even if there are no legal restrictions, you should never, ever try to slip something past the guest.

We cannot abuse our guests the way some other industries do. Repeat patronage is our lifeblood. If we get too cute, our cover counts will immediately drop like a rock. That's usually not the case for other service industries. For instance, if the person who fixes your garage door does a terrible job, you tell him or her to get lost. But unlike a restaurant experience, you would rarely take the time to spread this around to your friends and acquaintances.

PURCHASING'S LINK TO THE REST OF THE RESTAURANT

Throughout this book we will talk quite a bit about purchasing's impact on some of the day-to-day activities performed by the typical restaurant operation. As you read this book, consider how a decision about purchasing can affect every other part of the restaurant.

There are eleven categories of menu misrepresentation that must be avoided. These were originally introduced by the **National Restaurant Association (NRA)** in its 1977 classic work, *Accuracy in Menus*. In fact, even today menu-planning textbooks and various restaurant and foodservice associations articulate these guidelines. (See, e.g., The Canadian Restaurant and Foodservices Association Web site http://www.crfa.ca/resourcecentre/foodsafety/policyandregulations/ accuracyinmenus.asp.) In fact, it wouldn't surprise us if one of the textbooks currently on your desk or on your bookshelf contains this information.

1. *Quantity.* Any size information you include on the menu must be accurate. For instance, you can't say "extra large" eggs unless you are using this size as defined by the U.S. government. Similarly, if you like to use terminology, such as *supersize,* you might consider an additional descriptor noting the exact weight or volume of product served.

2. *Quality.* This is one of our biggest problems. We just can't stop saying "prime rib," even though we may be serving a USDA Choice grade of beef. Sometimes it's easy to fall into this trap unknowingly. For instance, someone may not know that a chopped and reformed, pressed beef product, such as sliced "pastrami," is not the same as the real thing.

3. *Price.* This may come into play when you are using a *market-pricing technique,* where you don't list a price on the menu, but rely on the server to quote it correctly at tableside. It also crops up if, for example, you have a policy of charging a bit more for all-white-meat chicken dinners, or for substituting a baked potato for rice, but fail to disclose these policies to the guest. In our experience, one of

the biggest problems is when you charge for beverage refills, but don't state that clearly on the menu. Another one
we see all the time is the server who asks if the table wants
bottled water without telling guests that there's a charge
for it. It seems to us that asking guests to choose between
tap water and bottled water is not enough to warn many
of them that they'll get hit with an extra charge.

4. *Brand name.* A lot of us can't seem to remember that
Jell-O is a **brand name,** and we can't use it on the menu
if we are serving a no-name gelatin. We do better with
things like soda pop, where we typically inform the guest
that, "We don't have Coke; is Pepsi OK?"

5. *Product identification.* The U.S. government has established
standards of identity for several food and beverage products. A standard of identity defines what a product must be
in order to be called by its standard name. For instance,
there is a big difference between maple syrup and maple-
flavored syrup. It is easy to unknowingly puff up the menu
description with incorrect and/or misleading terminology.

6. *Point of origin.* This is another area where we tend to toss
around incorrect terminology without giving it a second
thought. For instance, *Colorado beef* sounds a lot nicer
than just plain beef. But as you know, the point of origin
can have a substantial effect on the culinary quality, taste,
and/or texture of foods and beverages. Guests these days
are also more aware of these distinctions.

7. *Merchandising terms.* Sometimes we get carried away
when we work on a menu project in culinary school.
Terms like *center-cut pork chops, made from scratch, home
made,* are all over the page. That's OK when you're developing a menu in class. The problem comes when we can't
break this habit when preparing live menus.

8. *Preservation.* Be careful when using the term *fresh.* Some
day you may have to use a frozen product because the
fresh one is unavailable. You might get away with using
terms like *freshly prepared* or *prepared to order,* but we
recommend not pushing the issue. Never give the impression that something's fresh when in fact it has been frozen,
canned, bottled, or dried. And never, ever serve a slacked-
out product (i.e., a thawed, previously frozen item palmed
off as fresh).

9. *Means of preparation.* Several guests select menu items because of the way they are prepared. For instance, some folks go to Burger King because they like a broiled hamburger, whereas some others go to Wendy's because they prefer the fried. Some guests may be on diets that prohibit fried items, so if you list a broiled menu item but serve it fried, they will be very upset.

A related issue is listing the type of ingredients used in a menu item. If you say that your potatoes are fried in canola oil you could jeopardize someone's health if you substitute another type of fat.

10. *Illustrations/graphics.* We have two words about using pictures on menus or menu boards: forget it. You can't possibly make the item look like the picture. We realize that pictures are critical marketing components of quick-service operations, but even so, we don't like them. It would be much better, and safer, to prepare a few sample plates and display them in the entry area. At least these are realistic. Plus, they can enhance your overall marketing efforts.

11. *Nutrition.* Since about the mid-1990s, U.S. restaurants have been required to verify any health or dietary claims made on the menu. Our answer to that: Don't make any. Go ahead and list ingredients if you want to, but stay away from the nutritional sciences unless the initials after your name are RD (registered dietician) or you're willing to pay one to do a nutritional workup that you can list on a brochure, menu, or company Web site. We prefer letting the consumers draw their own conclusions. If they are concerned about healthy eating they will know what to order and what to stay away from. Your main duty is to make sure that the ingredients you list are actually the ones you're using.

TYPES OF MENUS

There are many types of food and beverage menus, enough to satisfy just about every need you may have. The menu needs to tell the customer what is available, when it's available, and at what price. Menus are also presented in different formats. Let's review some of the more common ones used in today's restaurant industry

■ WHAT FOOD IS AVAILABLE, AND WHEN

Some menus never change; the same items are available for lunch and dinner. Whatever is offered on Tuesday is offered on Wednesday.

Some menus are connected to timing. The meal part (day part) menu focuses on a particular meal, or part of the day. For instance, it may be a menu used only for breakfast, lunch, dinner, high tea, and so on.

A cycle menu repeats itself according to a predetermined pattern. It usually has a few items on it that do not change; however, it will contain several different items each day in addition to the permanent ones. For instance, on Mondays you may serve pasta specials, Tuesdays may call for salad specials, and so on. This type of menu is typically used in noncommercial food services, such as assisted living centers, or in some commercial ones, such as cruise lines. It is most common whenever you are serving a captive audience that could become bored with the same old thing every day.

Some establishments offer a daily menu. Given the proliferation and convenience of desktop publishing, you could easily print a new menu every day and slip it into a fancy, permanent binder. More likely, you would print one that contains several standardized items, but also includes highlighted specials. For instance, a seafood house could have its daily catches highlighted at the top of the menu, or a microbrewery might list its beer specials in a daily menu insert. A special-occasion menu is a form of daily menu. For instance, you may want to create something different for Thanksgiving, Mother's Day, or Christmas.

Limited menus do not offer as many items as other menus. One example is a down-time menu. This is usually a menu that offers only a few items. It is normally used whenever you must be open but do not expect very many guests. However, there may be opportunities to boost sales revenue during these slow periods if you offer a few food options to guests. For instance, an early-bird menu, or a night-owl menu for the lounge, can bring in quite a few dollars without increasing your labor or overhead substantially. The early-bird menu is typically a scaled-down version of the regular menu(s). The chef usually picks a few items that will appeal to diners who don't mind visiting during off-hours, say from 4:00 p.m. to 6:00 p.m. In most situations, the menu prices are lower than normal. The portion sizes may also be a bit smaller.

The casual menu is the most typical type of limited menu. It is similar to the down-time menu, but it is not priced as low—plus, it typically offers a bigger selection. It is the perfect menu for places that have small kitchens but large lounges and dining rooms, where speed is essential.

■ PRICING

Another way of categorizing menus is by pricing. An a la carte menu lists a price for every item. Guests pay a separate price for every dish ordered. There are no "combo" meals or "value" meals. Nothing comes with the entrée but the table setting—and if it's a fast-food restaurant the guests might have to fetch those themselves.

A fixed-price menu, sometimes referred to as a bundled, *prix fixe,* all-inclusive, *table d'hote,* taster, or chef's tasting and paired wines menu, is the opposite of an a la carte menu. There is one price for a set meal or set combination of food and beverage items.

Café menus are used by some high-end restaurants that want to offer patrons a choice between the regular (higher-priced) menu in the main dining room and a limited (lower-priced) menu in a separate area. It is similar to what you might find in celebrity chef Wolfgang Puck's Spago's, where there may be a café up front with a formal dining area in the back, or off to the side.

■ MENU FORMATS

Menus are also presented in different formats. Menus are not always printed on heavy paper and handed to the customer. Another popular format is the tabletop menu. This type of menu is oftentimes referred to as a table-top display or a table tent. It is used primarily to promote your money makers. The problem seems to be that guests don't usually read them. Or, if they do, they usually read them after they have given their orders to the server.

There is also the menu board or chalkboard. Think of this as a tabletop menu on steroids. A menu board is necessary if you operate a quick service facility and may also be required if you have a separate take-out area in your full-service restaurant. The chalkboard is popular in restaurants that wish to convey a European image. Like the typical table tent, though, guests usually don't read them completely until after they put in their orders.

Some restaurants offer verbal menus. Many properties have their servers recite the food specials of the day at tableside. We prefer a printed menu insert instead of the time-consuming speech. Guests are usually chatting away and aren't always eager to sit still long enough to hear the full spiel.

Restaurants that offer interactive menus allow guests to mix and match their orders. For instance, in some Italian restaurants guests can select the type of pasta they want, the type of sauce, and so on.

You also might see this with some "bingo" catering menus. These menus have several lists of food and beverage items, whereby the client picks, say, number 3 from column A, number 21 from column B, and so forth. Eventually he or she ends up with a personalized menu for the event.

Some restaurants use wireless technology (WIFI) to display their wine lists. Sometimes a computer terminal is installed at each table. Or the floor manager brings a laptop to the table. Guests can interact, for example, by entering their desired entrees into the system and waiting for the computer to make wine suggestions.

Another format is the chef's menu. This is the one you spring on people who don't want to see a menu. They say, "Let the chef order for me." There are three ways to go: You can ask the customer to give you some advance notice about what he or she wants, and then have those things ready upon arrival; you let the guest decide, or you can select items from your current menu(s). A third alternative is for you to put something unique together, something that doesn't appear on the regular menu(s). A potential downside of options 1 and 3 is you have to price them quickly; you need to know your numbers, as the bookkeeper may not be around. And you would need to know if you have enough food items and the right wines to pair with them, or if you have to make a special run to the vendor in order to get what you need.

▒ SPECIAL MENUS

Some restaurants offer special menus for specific items. For example, there might be a drink list. High-end restaurants typically offer a separate wine list, specialty cocktail list, after-dinner drink list, waters list, and so on. While the typical chef does not plan these types of menus, he or she should be involved in their development to some degree to ensure that the food menus will complement them.

Some properties offer dessert menus. This type of menu offers great upselling opportunities. Some dessert menus include suggested after-dinner drinks. Sometimes there are no printed dessert menus; instead, the "menu" consists of sample desserts showcased on a dessert cart or dessert tray.

There are also menus used for foodservice establishments besides restaurants. Hotels sometimes offer room-service menus, which typically contain a sampling of the food items offered in the hotel's other food outlets. In high-end properties the room-service menu may also include a notation that the hotel will try to give the guest anything on the hotel restaurant's menus, even those items not listed on the room-service menu.

If you offer on-premise or off-premise catering options, you may want to have separate catering menus, or you may prefer to work with clients to create something from scratch. Building from scratch is more time-consuming; however, preprinted menus are typically viewed by guests who are not on your property. You will not be there to help them and to guide them. By the way, if you offer catering services, make sure to highlight this fact on your restaurant menu and on any other promotional materials you use.

KNOW THY GUEST

We repeat: Before you buy anything you have to know what you're planning to sell. And what you sell has to be consistent with your target market's desires. If you have a good handle on your customer base, you will be able to develop the appropriate menu(s) and the best possible combination of food and beverage items to include on them. Once that is done, you are ready to take the next step: the preparation of standard recipes and standard product specifications. With that said, it's time to determine the quality and other characteristics of everything the guest will experience.

APPLY WHAT YOU'VE LEARNED

1. You have recently acquired a small corner lot property to lease for your newest venture. The concept is an upscale, fast-paced coffeehouse, catered toward high-income Manhattan consumers.

You also intend to offer breakfast and brunch catering in the Lower West Side area for groups of up to 50 people. Give an example of what you think might be your ten top-selling food items, five top-selling beverages, and at least one nonfood or beverage item. Describe how profitable these items might be for your new venture, and make a list of purchases you will need to provide these menu items to your consumer.

2. You were recently hired as executive chef for a casual neighborhood bar in a well-known area near your home. The operating hours are from 5 p.m. to 2 a.m. last call, and it typically closes around 3:30 a.m. Answer each of the following questions in one or two sentences:

a. Give an example of your target customer.

b. What experience do these customers expect in your bar?

c. What beverages and foods should your bar offer to them?

d. Draw up a preliminary, one-page menu for this concept.

DISCUSSION QUESTIONS

1. Name three major areas that impact what a foodservice operation sells.

2. Name five categories of menu misrepresentation that the NRA advises should be avoided.

3. Give examples of how a restaurant might misrepresent the menu in each of the eleven categories noted by the NRA.

4. Name ten types of food and beverage menus, and briefly describe them in your own words.

PURCHASE ORDER

No. 28852

SHOW THIS NUMBER

...ES, REFERENCES...VOICES, B/L'S OR CORRESPONDENCE PERTAINING TO THIS ORDER

ZIP CODE

ZIP CODE

...TY & STA...

UNIT PRICE

DATE REQUIRED

DESCRIPTION

UNIT

2

PRODUCT
QUALITY

What Kind of Stuff Should I Buy?

CHAPTER OUTLINE

- SPECIFICATIONS
- EXAMPLE SPECIFICATIONS

LEARNING OBJECTIVES

☑ Standardize a recipe.

☑ Identify the consequences of not standardizing recipes.

☑ Define the terms *product identification* and *spec*.

☑ Identify the most common components of a product specification.

☑ Discuss the difference between quality and wholesomeness.

☑ Describe product quality to purveyors.

☑ Troubleshoot a product specification sheet and evaluate its comprehensiveness.

The types of foods and beverages you purchase cannot be determined until you develop standardized recipes. If you work for a large company, chances are this task has been done for you. But even then, you may be responsible for developing standardized recipes for the daily specials, the catering options, and so forth.

Standardized recipes are absolutely essential. This doesn't mean that you can't be creative, or that you cannot let your sous chef or other food handlers be creative. Be as creative as you want. Come up with different things now and then. Guests expect that.

However, when a new item is developed, it is essential that you have it standardized in your recipe file. Unless it's standardized you cannot have it costed out and priced properly; you then have a gap in your cost control system. And without a standardized recipe you have no quality control guideline for that item. Furthermore, what would happen if the person who created the recipe suddenly quit, leaving you without the ability to offer that item again?

If you don't have standardized recipes, stop reading and devote your time to completing that critical work. If you think you have standardized recipes, review them once more before you continue with this book. We see a lot of so-called standardized recipes that aren't accurate. If you don't believe us, pick up any food magazine and try to prepare some of the recipes. For instance, a recipe might call for "milk." What kind of milk? What brand name and/or U.S. government grade? Or it might say, "chop up one onion." What kind of onion? How big? What type of cut? This is where cost and quality control go out the window. You might be able to get away with that when you're cooking at home, but you cannot afford this type of ambiguity in today's competitive restaurant environment.

But enough about standardized recipes. You get plenty of that in culinary school, or in an apprentice program, or on the job. Let's move to the next step: product specifications.

SPECIFICATIONS

One of your biggest responsibilities is to determine exactly what you want to purchase before you start shopping around. That means you, or someone else in the company, must take the time to develop product specifications for all the ingredients you intend to purchase.

If you, or another company manager, fail to prepare the specifications, then your **purveyors**—your **vendors**—will. When you put in an order, say, for onions and the purveyor has to ask you all sorts of questions (e.g., What are you going to use them for? What type of onion would you like? How big do you want the onion to be?) before your order can be filled, someone in your company is falling down on the job. Purveyors love it when you let them determine the specifications. Except for **panic buying** (where you're in a pinch and will pay any price to get the stuff right now!), it's about as good as it gets for them.

You must be in control when you're ordering any type of food, beverage, nonfood item, or outside contract service. You do not want the purveyors to call the shots. Not only will you lose money with this strategy, you risk having the purveyors influence what kinds of things you will use in your restaurant. It's OK to talk with sales reps to solicit product information, but don't let them take over the driver's seat.

A **product specification,** sometimes referred to as **product identification, specification,** or *spec,* is a description of all the characteristics in a product required to fill certain production and/or service needs. It should include product information that can be verified upon delivery and that can be communicated easily from you to the various purveyors you need to work with. Good specifications typically include some or all of the following characteristics:

- ☑ Intended use
- ☑ Exact name
- ☑ Product quality
- ☑ Product size
- ☑ Yield
- ☑ Packaging
- ☑ Preservation and/or processing method
- ☑ Point of origin
- ☑ Product color
- ☑ Ripeness or age
- ☑ Product form
- ☑ Expiration date
- ☑ Approved substitutes
- ☑ Other information

The specs will tell you everything you need to know about a product, from how it got here to how long it can be left in storage. Your specs need to tell you and your vendor not only the size of the Yukon Gold potatoes you need to buy when your menu features Rosemary Chicken on a Bed of Potatoes, but that if Yukon Golds aren't available, Red Bliss potatoes can be used. Let's take a closer look at the listed characteristics and why each is so important.

■ INTENDED USE

We consider **intended use** the most critical piece of information. You need to know exactly what you're going to do with an item before you prepare the rest of the specification. For instance, a specification for mustard will vary, depending on how you intend to use it. If you want to use it in recipes, perhaps a **bulk pack** of mustard is sufficient, whereas if you want to use it as a room-service condiment, you may wish to purchase small, single-serve bottles.

■ EXACT NAME

You don't just want milk. You want "2 percent fluid milk." Or you want "nonfat dried milk." Or you want "soy milk." If you have adequately standardized recipes, they will have the exact name of each ingredient. You must make sure that you order the right item, or else the recipe won't work. The same thing is true for things like dish machine chemicals; a substitute item may not work well, plus it may damage the machine.

■ PRODUCT QUALITY

You can't tell purveyors that you want to order a "quality" product. This is meaningless. You must tell them what kind of quality, as there are several variations. For instance, most purveyors carry three quality levels: good, better, and best. The quality you want, or need, will be determined by the intended use of the product.

Don't confuse quality with wholesomeness. All levels of quality are wholesome. But for a product to advance from the good level to the best level, it must have a very attractive appearance. Higher-quality items score very well on appearance factors and will usually look great. You will pay more for that look, though. Good-quality products may be sufficient if they will be chopped up and disguised in a recipe, whereas center-plate items may call for better or best quality. Moral of the story: Don't purchase expensive higher qualities unless they are absolutely necessary.

Your desired quality can be communicated to purveyors in several ways. You can (1) use U.S. government grades; (2) use brand names; and/or (3) for items that have no brand names or government grades, develop your own standard of quality and trust that the purveyors will adhere to it when they supply an inventory of products they feel will meet your needs.

Brand names are probably the most useful statement of quality. Many items carry recognizable brand names and are very consistent. This is especially true for premium brands. It is also true for purveyors that carry several **packers' brands** under the brand name umbrella.

Packers' brands are similar to government grades. In effect, the purveyor has created a personal grading system that is used instead of the government grading system. For instance, the word *Sysco* is a brand name, but the terms *Sysco Imperial, Sysco Classic, Sysco Reliance,* and *Sysco Value Line* are the Sysco Company's packers' brand names (i.e., packer's "grades"). One of the nice things about using **grading factors** like this is that, unlike U.S. government grades that refer to only the quality of the product, they typically also tell you something about other characteristics, for instance, the type of packaging the product comes in.

Many items carry a U.S. government grade. For some products, such as fresh produce, meats, and poultry, these grades are good indications of quality. However, since government grading is primarily a voluntary procedure, and the vendor has to pay for it, some purveyors may not carry U.S. graded merchandise. In fact, one of the primary reasons packers' brands came into existence was to avoid this expense. You can get around this problem, though, by stating on the specification that you require a certain government grade, but you will accept a nongraded item that is equivalent. Or you may accept something that is equivalent or better.

Some products do not have established government grading standards, nor do they carry recognizable brand names. This is especially common for most fish products. In this case, you need to develop your personal statement of quality. The easiest way to do this is to pull the information about these products from culinary textbooks. The sidebar includes some very good resources.

Jerry Chesser, *The Art and Science of Culinary Preparation* (Lansing, MI: Educational Institute of the AH&LA, 1992).

The Culinary Institute of America, *The Professional Chef,* 7th ed. (New York: Wiley, 2002).

Wayne Gisslen, *Professional Baking,* 4th ed. (New York: Wiley, 2005).

Wayne Gisslen, *Advanced Professional Cooking* (New York: Wiley, 1992).

Wayne Gisslen, *Professional Cooking,* 6th ed. (New York: Wiley, 2007).

▦ PRODUCT SIZE

This is not necessary for every item, but is for many of the things you buy. For some products, such as portion-cut meats, you can indicate an exact weight per piece. For others, such as large wholesale cuts of meat or whole chickens, usually you have to settle for a weight range. In other instances, the size of an item, such as lemons, shrimp, or lobster tails, is indicated by its **count,** that is, the number of items per case, per pound, or per 10 pounds. In the case with shrimp, for example, the U number—that is, the approximate number of pieces per pound—indicates the size. A U-20 shrimp indicates that there are "under" 20 pieces per pound.

▨ YIELD

For some products you may need to indicate the amount of **edible** (or **servable,** or **usable**) **yield** you'd prefer. For instance, you can usually buy lettuce that has 100% yield if you are willing to pay a high price for this type of convenience item. But you can also buy whole head lettuce that is less than 100 percent yield. If you buy whole lettuce, though, you want to make sure your purveyors know how much yield you expect. Alternately, you could indicate how much **waste,** or **trim,** you'll accept. Either way, it is important to make some statement about yield when you purchase whole, raw foods because the yield variations can be considerable among purveyors. There are also seasonal yield variations to contend with.

In the meat industry, yield is not as troublesome. Fresh or fresh frozen meats are pretty standardized. The **North American/Meat Processors Association (NAMP)** publication, *The Meat Buyers Guide,* contains yield grade information. There are comparable guides in other food categories, such as the **Produce Marketing Association's (PMA)** publication, *The PMA Fresh Produce Manual.* However, it is unusual to find a buyer's guide that contains the extensive amount of material included in the NAMP publication. In these cases it is up to you to obtain product samples from your purveyors and perform your own yield tests before deciding from whom to purchase.

▨ PACKAGING

This criterion has several dimensions. First of all, it's important to recognize that when we talk about packaging, for most products, we are not referring to how pretty the box is. Your main concern is the type of packaging products come in. In some cases, such as canned goods and dairy products, the type of packaging is standardized. But this is not the case with, say, many frozen items. Food processors that scrimp on packaging quality don't do you a favor. Even though the purchase price may be less, poor packaging will quickly compromise an item's culinary quality.

Another packaging consideration refers to the size of container that best fits your needs. For instance, you may prefer half-and-half in quart containers instead of pints.

For some food items, the way they are packed may be important. For instance, you may want cheese slices individually wrapped. You can't always assume that you will receive it this way from each purveyor.

Finally, many chefs want to buy from purveyors who use recycled packaging. They may also prefer doing business with purveyors who offer reusable packaging, such as the plastic tubs some vendors use to deliver fresh fish.

In our experience, one of the easiest ways purveyors can afford to cut their prices is to downgrade the packaging. But this is false economy. The things we use in the typical restaurant can suffer from a lot of rough handling. Poor packaging will increase the amount of waste to the point where it will be more expensive than paying a bit more up front for proper packaging.

▨ PRESERVATION AND/OR PROCESSING METHOD

For some products you will be able to choose different preservation methods. For instance, you could order refrigerated or frozen meats, canned or frozen green beans, and so on.

You also could specify unique types of processing methods, such as smoked fish, oil-cured olives, genetically altered tomatoes, and so forth.

The type of preservation and/or processing method selected often influences the taste and other culinary characteristics of finished menu items. Consequently, before you make any changes in this part of the spec, be sure that the recipes using these ingredients will not suffer.

▨ POINT OF ORIGIN

In some cases you need to indicate on the spec the exact part of the world that a food item should come from. The flavor, texture, and so forth of an item can differ dramatically among regions. It is also necessary to include this bit of information if you state on your menu that an item comes from a particular location; for instance, if it says Colorado beef on the menu, you must also list it on the spec.

A related issue is to indicate on the spec where a food item should *not* come from. For instance, for social or political reasons, your company may refuse to purchase products that come from areas that do not promote human rights. Or you may not wish to buy products produced in a country that does not protect the environment.

■ PRODUCT COLOR

Some items, such as bell peppers, are available in more than one color. If the exact name of the product does not include the color you must include it elsewhere on the spec.

■ RIPENESS OR AGE

This is especially important for fresh produce. Meats also need an indication of the amount of *age* you want the item to have. Some wines have a similar system that reflects, among other things, the year of production.

■ PRODUCT FORM

Product form is an important consideration for many processed items. For example, do you want your cheese in a brick, or would you rather have it sliced? Do you want your roast beef pre-cooked, or should it be raw? Usually the exact name of the product will include its form, but if it doesn't, you will have to indicate it elsewhere on the spec.

■ EXPIRATION DATE

Many product labels list **pull dates, sell-by dates, best-if-used-by dates,** or **freshness dates.** You must reference these dates somewhere on your spec. You cannot accept anything that will stay in your inventory after these dates. The culinary quality will be seriously compromised. And the health inspector will downgrade your establishment if he or she spots it on your premises.

▪ APPROVED SUBSTITUTES

Purveyors may not always have exactly what you want. However, they may have **approved substitutes** that will serve your needs. If you know for a fact that a substitute will work for you, then you might want to include it on the spec. But be very careful. Don't take the sales rep's word that a substitute will work. If a recipe, for instance, calls for a certain brand of butter, you should never use a different brand unless you've taken the time to test the substitute under actual operating conditions. You can't rely on the purveyor's tests that were probably conducted under ideal conditions in a food lab.

▪ OTHER INFORMATION

The previous information usually covers all the bases you need to touch when preparing specifications for everyday use. If, however, you anticipate preparing specs that will be used to solicit competitive bids from purveyors that will cover a long period of time, say six months or more, you should consider adding some non-product information. For instance, you should indicate such things as these:

☑ Testing and inspection procedures you will use when receiving the items

☑ Amount of product you expect to purchase over the contract period

☑ Delivery procedures desired

☑ Expected credit and payment terms

☑ Whether the products must be available to all units of the restaurant chain

☑ Instructions to bidders detailing the bid procedures, your vendor selection criteria, and the qualifications and capabilities you expect purveyors to have

It is not always cost-effective for the typical restaurant to engage in long-term, competitive **bid buying,** because the amounts purchased are usually too small to interest most vendors. Also, if you make a mistake during the process, you will have to live with your errors for the contract's duration. Although you can get a better deal when you buy in bulk, you should do so only if you have the time

PURCHASING'S LINK TO HUMAN RESOURCES (HR)

Many job classifications in the restaurant require some sort of purchasing and/or inventory control skill. Purchasing should interact closely with HR to ensure that these activities are included in the pertinent job descriptions. Training is another HR activity that purchasing may be called upon to do. For instance, the chef may be the one to perform cuttings and other demos for the service staff. Or he or she may be the one who helps train new hires who do not work in the kitchens, but need to have some product knowledge that only the chef can provide.

and expertise to anticipate every problem and deal with it before you sign the contract. For most of us, it may be cheaper in the long run to buy day to day. If you purchase daily and you have a bad experience with a particular purveyor, you can dump the offender easily and find someone else since you are not stuck with a long-term contract.

EXAMPLE SPECIFICATIONS

Following is a specification outline and an example specification for each of the major food and beverage product categories you purchase. If you have some time to spare, use the specification outlines to prepare a few specs. Keep in mind that you don't necessarily have to complete the entire outline for every product. You need only work on the pertinent areas. For instance, **point of origin, product size,** and color may be immaterial for something like canned tomato juice. Formatting of specs may vary, but it's important to include all relevant information.

Exact name
Intended use
Quality standard
Product size
Yield
Size of container
Type of packaging
Packaging procedure
Minimum weight per case
Preservation method
Point of origin
Color
Degree of ripeness
Product form

A SPECIFICATION OUTLINE FOR FRESH PRODUCE PRODUCTS

Iceberg lettuce
Used for tossed salad
U.S. No. 1 grade (high end) (or equivalent)
10-pound poly pack
Chopped lettuce
Fresh, refrigerated
Fully ripened

AN EXAMPLE OF A FRESH PRODUCE PRODUCT SPECIFICATION

Exact name
Intended use
Quality standard
Product size
Drained weight (yield)
Size of container
Type of packaging
Packaging procedure
Packing medium
Type of processing
Color
Product form

A SPECIFICATION OUTLINE FOR GROCERY PRODUCTS

Pineapple slices
Used for salad bar
Dole brand (or equivalent)
66 count
Packed in No. 10 can
Packed in unsweetened pineapple juice

AN EXAMPLE OF A GROCERY PRODUCT SPECIFICATION

Exact name
Intended use
Quality standard
Product size
Yield
Size of container
Type of packaging
Packaging procedure
Preservation method
Product form

A SPECIFICATION OUTLINE FOR DAIRY PRODUCTS

Butter
Used for customer service
U.S. Grade AA (or equivalent)
Butter chips
90 count
Chips individually wrapped in moisture-proof, vapor-proof material
5-pound waxed box
Refrigerated

AN EXAMPLE OF A DAIRY PRODUCT SPECIFICATION

Exact name
Intended use
Quality standard
Product size
Size of container
Type of packaging
Packaging procedure
Preservation method
Color
Product form

A SPECIFICATION OUTLINE FOR EGG PRODUCTS

Scrambled egg mix
Used on buffet
Fresh Start brand (or equivalent)
2-pound moisture-proof, vapor-proof carton
Packed 6 cartons per case
Refrigerated liquid

AN EXAMPLE OF AN EGG PRODUCT SPECIFICATION

Exact name
Intended use
Quality standard
Product size
Yield
Size of container
Type of packaging
Packaging procedure
Preservation method
Product form

A SPECIFICATION OUTLINE FOR POULTRY PRODUCTS

Boneless, skinless chicken breast, raw
Used for dinner entrées
Tyson brand (or equivalent)
Packed 48, 4-ounce portions per case
Packed in moisture-proof, vapor-proof container
Layered in plastic cell-pack inserts
Fresh frozen

AN EXAMPLE OF A POULTRY PRODUCT SPECIFICATION

Exact name
Intended use
Quality standard
Packed Under Federal Inspection (PUFI)
Product size
Yield
Size of container
Type of packaging
Packaging procedure
Packing medium
Preservation method
Point of origin
Product form

A SPECIFICATION OUTLINE FOR FISH PRODUCTS

Tuna, solid white, albacore
Used to prepare tuna salad
Chicken of the Sea brand (or equivalent)
Water pack
Packed in $66\frac{1}{2}$ ounce can
Packed 6 cans per case
Moisture-proof case

AN EXAMPLE OF A FISH PRODUCT SPECIFICATION

Exact name
Intended use
Quality standard
Product size
Yield
Size of container
Type of packaging
Packaging procedure
Preservation method
Point of origin
Tenderization method
Product form

A SPECIFICATION OUTLINE FOR MEAT PRODUCTS

New York strip steak
Used for dinner entrée
Meat Buyer's Guide (MBG) No. 1180
USDA Choice Grade (high end) (or equivalent)
Cut from USDA Yield Grade 2 carcass (or equivalent)
Dry aged 14 to 21 days
12-ounce portion cut
Individually wrapped in plastic film
Layered in 10- to 12-pound moisture-proof case
Refrigerated

AN EXAMPLE OF A MEAT PRODUCT SPECIFICATION

Exact name
Intended use
Brand name
Size of container
Type of container
Preservation method
Point of origin
Vintage
Alcohol content

A SPECIFICATION OUTLINE FOR BEVERAGE ALCOHOL PRODUCTS

Vodka
Used for drink service at the service bar
Used in the service bar's automatic drink dispenser
Smirnoff brand (or equivalent)
80 proof
1.50 liter, or 1.75 liter, glass bottle

AN EXAMPLE OF A BEVERAGE ALCOHOL PRODUCT SPECIFICATION

Exact name
Intended use
Quality standard
Size of container
Type of container
Preservation method
Product form

A SPECIFICATION OUTLINE FOR NONALCOHOLIC BEVERAGE PRODUCTS

Cola: regular; diet; regular-caffeine free; diet caffeine-free
Used for drink service in lounge, service bar, and dining room
Coca Cola brand
5-gallon bag-in-the-box pack
Postmix syrup

AN EXAMPLE OF A NONALCOHOLIC BEVERAGE PRODUCT SPECIFICATION

APPLY WHAT YOU'VE LEARNED

1. Your line cooks have been bugging you for months to get a food processor for the restaurant. They currently use blenders to puree all the soups, sauces, and other items. They've gone through three industrial blenders in the past year. With an overall smallwares budget of $1,000 per year, what type of processor would you consider purchasing? Provide sources for your decision—including, but not limited to, Internet printouts, store flyers, advertisements, documentation from foodservice operations, or vendors. Make clear what financial and operational benefits your plan has.

2. You have a full-time staff of 20 who provide fresh-from-scratch items for your daily dinner menu. Unfortunately, health insurance costs skyrocketed, and you will have to replace 10 full-time employees with less-experienced part-time workers. Instead of butchering your meats in-house, you decide to purchase preportioned shrink-wrapped meats. What purchasing issues might this decision affect? Discuss both positive and negative things.

DISCUSSION QUESTIONS

1. What type of information must an F & B professional have before determining the types of foods and beverages to purchase? Why?

2. What does it mean to standardize a recipe?

3. Look at the following list of ingredients from a recipe for Lemon-Berry Trifle. What are some of its trouble spots regarding standardization? What questions might come up when reading it?

Lemon-Berry Trifle

8 egg yolks
1 cup sugar
4 lemons, juiced
1 stick of butter, cut in chunks
3 pints berries
1 ½ cups whipped cream
2 rounds of yellow cake, cubed and toasted

4. What is a spec? What other terms mean the same thing?

5. What should a spec include? What are some characteristics of a spec?

6. Who typically decides what information to include on the product specifications if a manager in the operation doesn't?

7. Do quality and wholesomeness refer to the same thing? Why or why not?

8. How can you let purveyors know what quality of a product you want?

9. What type of other information might a product specification include? Name two or three examples.

10. Does every product specification have to include all of the suggested characteristics? Why or why not?

11. Look at the sample product specification for Muy Fresco Dispenser Cheddar Cheese Sauce available online from Advanced Food Products, LLC (http://www.afpllc.com/pdf/ CHEDFITMENTLESS.PDF#search='product%20specification %20food'). Does this spec include all of the characteristics noted in the text? What other information does this spec include? Why do you think these extras are included?

12. Is competitive bid buying always cost-effective for restaurants?

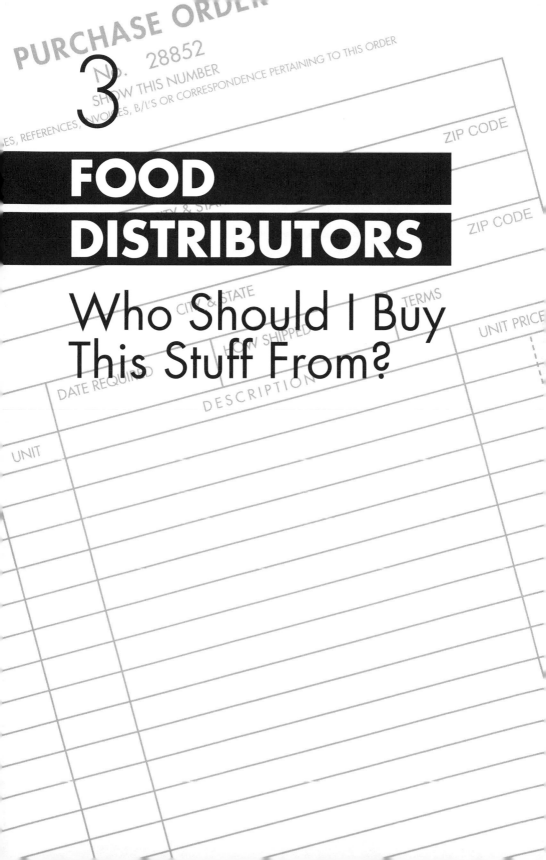

PURCHASE ORDER

NO. 28852

SHOW THIS NUMBER

ES, REFERENCES, INVOICES, B/L'S OR CORRESPONDENCE PERTAINING TO THIS ORDER

ZIP CODE

3

FOOD DISTRIBUTORS

Who Should I Buy This Stuff From?

CHAPTER OUTLINE

- VENDOR-SELECTION CRITERIA
- OVERALL VALUE

LEARNING OBJECTIVES

☑ Understand how methods used to select a vendor affect an F & B operation's cost of sales.

☑ Develop selection criteria based on the operation's needs.

☑ Investigate potential suppliers and assess their overall fit to the operation.

☑ Discuss the implications of various pricing systems, ordering procedures, and credit terms.

☑ Describe perceived value and its relation to product quality.

☑ Describe the difference between AP price and EP cost.

Your vendors are like your employees; you have to depend on them to take care of you. And you have to trust that they'll do that day in and day out. But unlike employees, you can't watch over them all the time. Selecting purveyors and keeping track of their work is a tall order, but we suppose if our chosen profession were easy, anyone could do it.

Your cost of sales begins right here, at vendor selection. This is where the cost is set. You must have the discipline and the dedication to check out the available vendors and dig into their backgrounds before spending money with them. If you don't do that you will forever be playing the trial and error game, shifting from one vendor to another seeking the best possible value. This strategy may be acceptable if you are not tied to a long-term contract. However, it can be just as time-consuming as doing your homework about purveyors in the first place. We don't recommend going down this road because the vendors are better at this game than we are. We prefer testing the water before jumping in.

If you are part of a national chain operation, then your vendor-selection task will be much easier. Typically, these organizations have a centralized purchasing department that, among other things, develops specifications and an approved supplier list for all restaurants to use. The central office does most of the legwork. It may also set up some long-term pricing arrangements that you can tap into.

But even though a chain restaurant may have the advantages of centralized purchasing support, the local restaurant chef must still do some selection because it is not normal for the central buyers to select every possible vendor. On one hand, for instance, you will usually have to select your own local dairy purveyor as well as the local laundry and linen service. On the other hand, even though you may have to do some research on local vendors, the central office can help you by giving you expert guidance as well as little tips you can use to make the process easier and more effective. It's like having a co-pilot who knows more about flying than you do.

Although the central corporate support you can get with the chain organizations doesn't come cheap, it is a welcome amenity. And in the long run, you may recover many times over the cost of belonging to a multiunit company.

For some products, you don't have too many vendor choices. For instance, there aren't very many dairy purveyors and laundry and linen services floating around in your area. Also, some vendors, such as soft drink companies, have exclusive selling arrangements that give them the sole right to sell a certain product line. In a case like this, you have only two options: take it or leave it.

VENDOR-SELECTION CRITERIA

When checking out potential vendors, consider some of the following attributes:

1. References

2. Compatibility/Chemistry

3. Size of the Firm

4. Location

5. Delivery Schedule

6. Storage Availability

7. Free Samples

8. Social Responsibility

9. Lead Time

10. Returns Policy

11. Minimum Order Requirements

12. Purveyor's Experience

13. Technological Capability

14. Ordering Procedures

15. Reciprocal Buying

16. Willingness to Barter

17. Cooperation in Bid Procedures

18. Long-Term Contracts

19. Credit Terms

20. Cost-Plus Purchasing

21. One-Stop Shopping

22. Standing Orders

23. Vendor's Consulting Support

▓ REFERENCES

Take the time to join local restaurant associations, or the local branch of the American Culinary Federation (ACF), or other similar business associations. This is where you will meet people who can share useful information about vendors who operate in your local market. If you're considering buying from a particular vendor, conduct a **reference check** to confirm the vendor's credentials. Also, ask business acquaintances these questions:

☑ Is this vendor fair? Honest? Does it strive to earn a fair profit while simultaneously handling client needs quickly and efficiently?

☑ Have you had any trouble with the drivers? Are they trustworthy, or should you plan to watch them carefully when receiving shipments?

☑ Are deliveries on time? How many times do you have to return shipments, or partial shipments? What is the **fill rate?**
(The fill rate is equal to the number of items delivered ÷
the number ordered × 100. If the fill rate isn't close to 100
percent, there are too many back orders.)

☑ Does the vendor credit your account immediately if you
have to return anything?

☑ Do the price quotations on the Internet, or those you get
over the phone or from distributor sales reps (DSR), match
the prices you see on the invoices? Are the product qualities
and other specification requirements consistent?

☑ Will he or she make emergency deliveries?

☑ What is the potential purveyor's financial strength? Is he or
she bonded adequately? (If the law in your area allows it,
you might consider running credit reports on all potential
purveyors; they can be very revealing.)

All of these questions will help you arrive at the answer to one
very important question: Is the vendor dependable? Dependability
is probably the most crucial attribute you seek. Remember, vendors
are like your employees; you must have confidence that they will
do the job right each and every time.

■ COMPATIBILITY/CHEMISTRY

When visiting with a potential vendor, do you get positive or
negative vibes? You don't have to love anyone, but you do have to
get along with everyone if you want to succeed in the service industry. Even though a purveyor may provide an adequate level of
service, sometimes you just can't get comfortable with that person,
or the company he or she represents. We humans are just naturally
attracted to some people more than others. This may not seem like
a big deal to you right now, but take our word for it: When there
is a serious problem with one of your orders, or a significant mis-
understanding, a good chemistry will help resolve the situation.
We're not suggesting you cave in and buy from purveyors who you
like regardless of how well they conduct business, but all other
things being equal, someone you can relate to is better than someone you can't stomach.

■ SIZE OF THE FIRM

If you do a lot of business, you must be assured that a purveyor is large enough to accommodate your needs. On the one hand, you must be certain that the products you need in order to operate properly are consistently available. On the other hand, large purveyors may be too impersonal for your taste; the vibes may be wrong. It's kind of a tricky dance; the business is unpredictable, and it is not always easy to find the right partner. You cannot afford too many missteps. Smaller, specialty vendors typically don't have the backup inventories that can be delivered to you at a moment's notice. If you prefer small, mom-and-pop vendors, know that you are risking more stockouts and, worst of all, the accompanying panic buying needed to fill a temporary shortage.

■ LOCATION

You would prefer all of your vendors to be nearby. The closer the better. This is critical, because every once in a while you or a member of your staff will need to go there to pick up something that you need right now. If you are a fan of **will-call** (i.e., **cash-and-carry**) **buying,** where you pick up your orders at a purveyor's warehouse, then closeness is a very significant benefit. In addition, it would also be nice if the purveyors were located between your home and the restaurant so that you could pick up things on your way to work.

■ DELIVERY SCHEDULE

You may not have much control over a purveyor's **delivery schedule** unless you are a gigantic restaurant company that swings a big checkbook. We all want morning deliveries. We certainly do not like anything showing up at the back door during the **sacred hours** of 11:30 a.m. to 1:30 p.m., but we don't think it's worthwhile to pay a premium for a customized delivery option. We would rather take on a bit of inconvenience, but not to the point where it interferes significantly with our production and service plans. The bottom line is this: Try to get deliveries when you know a knowledgeable person will be around and will have the time to receive and inspect the shipments. Another thing we suggest: If possible, stay away from purveyors who outsource their deliveries to common carriers. Such deliveries are called **drop shipments.** A common carrier can't help you if there is a problem with the shipment. You have to get back to the purveyor to resolve the problem; the driver can't take care of you right on the spot. This complicates an already complicated situation. Unfortunately, you usually have to accept a third-party delivery service for things you order on the Internet, though it's less of a problem if the purveyor uses FedEx, USPS, DHL, or UPS instead of some no-name delivery service.

■ STORAGE AVAILABILITY

Sometimes you run into a situation where you can get a very good deal, but only if you agree to buy and pay for a large order of merchandise. This is especially true for things like bottled water and paper products. This stuff is cheap when you can afford to buy a huge amount. But you then face the problem of where to store it. Some purveyors will let you take advantage of a **stockless purchase** plan, whereby you purchase the large amount, pay for it, but take delivery a little bit at a time. This is the best of both worlds; you get a generous discount, but don't have to worry about finding a place to store the inventory. Even if you have to pay a small carrying charge to the vendor to do this for you it's almost always a profitable transaction.

■ FREE SAMPLES

Most purveyors offer **free samples,** so this isn't usually a pertinent vendor-selection criterion. The main issue lies in your own restaurant, where there will be some managers who like free samples, the more the merrier, whereas there will be others who feel it can compromise you, especially if you take too many. We have no problem with free samples. A lot of the things you get aren't that expensive for the purveyor. The purveyor's out-of-pocket cost is less than the price charged to you. Furthermore, free samples are treated like any other sales and marketing expense. They are like any other business cost incurred by the vendor. Where you get into trouble, where the line is a little blurry, is when you start taking expensive things like tickets to the Super Bowl. That type of monkey business may cost you a lot more down the road. For instance, you may see your purveyor fudging a little here and there on product quality, packaging, and/or service if he or she is under pressure to recoup that type of marketing expense.

▩ SOCIAL RESPONSIBILITY

Some chefs and/or owners prefer to work with minority-owned and women-owned firms, or with those vendors who promote socially responsible agendas. For instance, some will not buy from purveyors who sell products manufactured by employees in countries who do not receive a basic level of wages or employee benefits. And some buyers will always make sure that at least one **socially responsible firm** is contacted whenever they shop around, especially if they are interested in contracting for a large amount of goods. For example, the MGM Mirage Corporation's diversity policies require that whenever purveyors bid for its business, at least one of them must be a minority-owned company. You can search the Internet for referral services that list these kinds of companies.

▩ LEAD TIME

Lead time is the time between when you order from a purveyor and when the shipment arrives. The shorter the lead time, the better. You prefer waiting until the last minute to make an order because you don't have to forecast your needs so far in advance. You can be more accurate. This will eventually have a favorable impact on your food and beverage costs by keeping your inventories at a manageable level.

▩ RETURNS POLICY

This can be a very sensitive issue. You should make sure you understand it clearly before you start ordering anything from a purveyor. Naturally, you want the most liberal **returns policy** you can get, but that is usually an unrealistic expectation. The reputable purveyors will not hassle you too much, but you can't take anything for granted. In our experience, the major problem is not so much that they refuse to take anything back, but the likelihood that they may want you to jump through too many hoops to get a credit posted to your account. We've also run into situations where we would have to pay to have the stuff picked up by the vendor, or pay UPS or FedEx to send it back. Worse, you may have to pay the vendor a huge **restocking fee** whenever you return something that isn't defective, but that you just found out you can't use, or if you try to return special-order merchandise. This is too costly and inconvenient. It's also hard on the F & B accountant who has to track these things. It's so much easier when the driver gives you a credit slip right then and there and takes the stuff back, or if a purveyor will fax or e-mail you a credit slip and pick up defective goods the next time the driver is in your area.

■ MINIMUM ORDER REQUIREMENTS

Before you can qualify for free delivery you usually must order a minimum dollar amount of goods. This is also true if you want to pick up things at the purveyor's warehouse on a will-call basis, although the **minimum order requirement** here will usually be much less. If you can't meet a potential purveyor's minimum order requirement you shouldn't increase your order sizes if it would create undue stress on your operation and your pocketbook. You should move on and keep searching. Alternately, you might consider modifying your menus, or shopping at **wholesale clubs,** like Sam's Club and Costco that are willing to sell smaller amounts.

■ PURVEYOR'S EXPERIENCE

You should be concerned with the amount of time a vendor has been in business. We're not crazy about buying from a vendor that's recently set up shop because we don't want to be the one it practices on. However, it would depend on what we're buying. If it's something pretty straightforward, no problem. And if we patronize **farmers' markets** for some items, we are fine with amateurs, since we think we know what we're doing and can tell the difference between high-quality, home-grown foods and the stuff that was picked up at the back dock of the local supermarket. But if the transaction is more complicated, or is a long-term contract, we prefer doing business with vendors who have a track record that we can check out. Furthermore, these vendors usually have all the kinks in their systems worked out and are, therefore, more dependable and predictable.

■ TECHNOLOGICAL CAPABILITY

These days, your purveyors should be accessible through the Internet. We would stay away from those who are *not* online unless it's absolutely necessary to deal with them in order to get exactly what we need. It's too inconvenient to deal with anyone who doesn't have an **e-procurement application** that you can access for information, such as product availability, new products, recipes, current promotions, and so on. You don't want to avoid all face-to-face contact with sales reps, as they are oftentimes good sources of restaurant trends and gossip, but in these days of high payroll and employee benefits costs, you need to take advantage of the efficiency that online ordering provides. For instance, knowing immediately that a product you want is unavailable is a big advantage. You can plan for a substitute or alternative right now and not have to wait until the driver shows up and tells you it's backordered.

■ ORDERING PROCEDURES

At first glance, **ordering procedures** might seem like a trivial issue. However, when you start shopping around, dealing with all sorts of vendors, it can become very difficult and costly to accommodate all different sorts of ordering procedures. This severely hampers your ability to look all over for the best possible deal. As with the delivery schedule issue, you should be partial to those vendors who most closely meet your needs. For instance, as already noted, you prefer doing business with those who offer online ordering capability. Too many ordering and delivery procedures create stress and confusion. It can also require you to adjust your receiving procedures too often, further pushing the stress-o-meter into the red zone. While it may be necessary for some things you buy, try to avoid spending too much time and energy adjusting to purveyors' unique needs if you don't have to.

■ RECIPROCAL BUYING

Roughly translated, **reciprocal buying** means, "I'll buy from you if you'll buy from me." It's not the greatest idea in the world. The best you can do is break even. And sooner or later the purveyor takes you for granted and does not provide acceptable supplier service. Unfortunately, sometimes your boss sets up this type of arrangement and you have to go along with it.

■ WILLINGNESS TO BARTER

Trade-outs are fairly common in our industry. Don't be afraid to ask potential purveyors if they are interested in **direct bartering** (i.e., will they trade with you one-on-one?). If you feel uncomfortable asking this question, search the Internet to find out if they belong to a

barter group—members who pay a fee for the privilege of being connected to other businesses who wish to earn and spend *trade dollars.* Some purveyors are very happy to accept free meals in lieu of cash payment. This is not a bad idea because it can save you quite a bit of out-of-pocket expense. If, for instance, you pay a $500 bill with $500 (retail value) of food and beverage, your out-of-pocket cost is only about $200. In our experience, few food vendors are interested in trading, and it's against the law for beverage alcohol companies to trade. Mostly, it's the service providers, such as billboard advertising companies, that like to do this with restaurants, hotels, and resorts.

■ COOPERATION IN BID PROCEDURES

Most purveyors realize that you are going to shop around, at least once in awhile. And most of them will respond to your **request for quote (RFQ).** However, you can't assume that all vendors are alike. Some may not want to spend the time with you if you are a small stop. And some might be so secretive that getting information out of them is like buying a car at a dealership. This is another reason why **online ordering** is so convenient and attractive; price and availability information is readily accessible. You don't have to wait until the sales rep "checks with the manager."

■ LONG-TERM CONTRACTS

Some purveyors are unwilling or unable to agree to price and/or product availability for the long term. The ones who will commit usually want to deal only with big stops, such as large multiunit restaurant companies. In this case, they typically offer **national contracts,** with **national distribution.** This type of contract covers the price each restaurant in the chain will pay, with the purveyor ensuring that all company restaurants will be able to purchase the product at their locations. If you want **long-term contracts,** your potential vendor list will be very short. If you find a purveyor willing to accommodate you, be very careful that you check out its track record, especially the financial history. You don't want to set up something with a vendor who doesn't have staying power.

■ CREDIT TERMS

Most vendors offer similar **credit terms,** so this may not be a pertinent criterion. However, you should always inquire about this, because you never know what they will agree to unless you ask. For instance, what type of financing do they offer? What does it cost?

What kind of discounts do they offer for prompt payment, **cash-on-delivery (COD) payment,** or payment in advance? What type of deposits do they require for special orders? For equipment? For reusable packaging, such as dairy crates and Cambro tubs used to deliver fish and poultry? How long is the credit period? Is it 30 days? 45 days? If the advantages offered by a vendor's credit terms exceed the amount of interest income you could earn on your money by hanging on to it as long as possible, you should take the credit line. But be careful that purveyors are not hiking their prices a little, or scrimping a little on product quality and service, in order to cover the cost of generous credit terms. They have to recoup that money somehow. This is why, for example, equipment leasing is not such a good idea in the long run, because while you hang on to your money for a long time, eventually you will pay much more for this advantage than you initially realized.

▦ COST-PLUS PURCHASING

Under **cost-plus buying,** the purchase price is equal to the purveyor's cost (sometimes referred to as the **landed cost**) plus a negotiated profit markup. The big restaurant companies have a love/hate relationship with this arrangement because, while it can help stabilize their food costs and make them more predictable, they can't help but wonder whether the purveyors are giving them truthful cost information. Alternately, vendors tend to shy away from this practice because they take on more risk. However, if the profit markup is a percentage, instead of a dollar amount, they may be willing to go along with it. If, for instance, you agree to a 10 percent profit markup, the purveyor loves it when the landed cost increases. It's similar to the local government that extracts a tax percentage on your utility bill. Since the tax is typically a percentage, they are in hog heaven when the basic price of electricity increases. If you get involved with cost-plus purchasing, first of all make sure that you can verify the landed costs. And second, never, never, never agree to a percentage. In fact, government-run foodservice operations are not allowed to negotiate for a percentage, but they can dicker for a dollar amount that stays the same no matter what happens to the landed cost.

▦ ONE-STOP SHOPPING

One-stop shopping (also referred to as **sole-source procurement, prime-vendor procurement, preferred-provider procurement,** or **single-source procurement**) is appealing to many chefs and owners because it's much easier to purchase as many products as you can from one vendor, or the fewest number of vendors. It is also easier and less labor-intensive to receive fewer shipments, store them, and so on. In addition, it cuts down on the paperwork you must process when you have several vendors. The idea is to do business with the least number of purveyors. This may cost you a bit more money in the long run, though, because you forgo the opportunity to shop around and uncover good deals. Also, there will be products in these vendors' catalogs that are not competitively priced. But if you're a small stop, one-stop shopping may be the preferred option. The little bit you can save from surfing the Internet and/or shopping all over town may not counterbalance the extra labor and administrative expense incurred if you switch back and forth among many purveyors. Plus, if you can guarantee that you will purchase approximately 90 percent of what you need from a single vendor, it will usually give you some price incentives. Unfortunately, to meet this 90 percent requirement you may have to adjust your menu(s) and other operating procedures so that they are consistent with the products carried by the preferred provider.

■ STANDING ORDERS

Under the **standing orders** procedure, a driver (usually referred to as a **route salesperson**) shows up, takes inventory of what you have, then takes off the truck enough product to bring you up to some predetermined par stock, enough to last until he or she visits you the next time. The driver writes up a **delivery ticket** (similar to an invoice) and gives you a copy, which you turn over to the bookkeeper. This is a common procedure for things like bread, dairy products, and soda pop syrup. A lot of chefs and owners love this arrangement and would love to have it for everything. It's very convenient. You don't have to forecast your needs far in advance, and the drivers do a lot of the work. It's a great idea, but you have to watch the drivers. Don't get too comfortable, or else you'll end up paying over and over for the same loaf of bread.

■ VENDOR'S CONSULTING SUPPORT

Vendors are a good source of product information, as well as other related information that can help you enhance your business. This is not a major issue for the big, multiunit restaurant companies; they are usually able to do this work themselves. But the small stops

---

PURCHASING'S LINK TO ACCOUNTING

Buyers will consistently provide cost data to the accounting department, data that are necessary for report preparation. The chef will also need to inform accounting if a new vendor should be added to the approved payee list. Furthermore, it is quite likely that the chef will contribute to the budgeting process.

---

are especially loyal to vendors who willingly share their expertise, provided these vendors don't give them advice that unfairly enhances the vendors' pocketbooks at their expense, such as providing them a suggested wine promotion that lists only stuff the vendor wants to get rid of. You can't know everything. And unless you are part of a large company that offers tech support, vendors are the logical information pipeline.

Some vendors are unable to provide this type of support, so you need to know that from the beginning. For instance, when purchasing kitchen equipment, some dealers stock it, sell it, and deliver it—period. Others can help you, say, secure the necessary health and/or building permits. You may have to pay more when you do business with vendors who have this capability, but unless you are a walking encyclopedia, you have to pay someone; it might as well be them.

OVERALL VALUE

The ultimate goal of vendor selection is to find those that offer the best possible value. This does not necessarily mean that you want only those vendors that have the lowest purchase prices. Value is much more than that. It has many dimensions.

They say that value, like beauty, is in the eye of the beholder. Maybe it's better to talk about *perceived value*. The perceived value of any product you buy is directly related to its quality and the types of additional services, sometimes referred to as **supplier services** or **support functions,** that come along with it. However, the perceived value is indirectly related to the cost you eventually pay for the product.

The cost is the **edible-portion (EP) cost** (or **servable cost,** or **usable cost**) of making the product ready-to-consume in your restaurant. It is not the **as-purchased (AP) price** of the product. As you probably know, you might pay a low AP price for a product, but by the time you trim all the waste and account for stealing, shrinkage, and other cooking loss, the EP cost may skyrocket. It's better to pay a little higher AP price if it results in the lowest-possible EP cost.

It's easier to talk about value when you restrict the discussion to AP price and EP cost. It's much more difficult to bring into the picture the quality- and support-function dimensions. For instance, if a vendor offers a product that is a higher quality than a comparable one offered by a competitor, and if both vendors charge the same AP price, the first vendor's value will be higher. However, this may not be important to you if the higher quality is immaterial. You may not want the higher quality, even though it's offered at the same AP price, because it could make other menu offerings pale in comparison. Guests may get confused. For instance, it might not be a good idea to serve top-of-the-line fresh vegetables if your center-plate items are lesser quality.

A similar situation can occur when two purveyors offer the same quality and the same AP price, but one of them offers additional support functions. If these additional support functions consist of suggested recipes developed by the vendor, you're reaction might be: Who cares? You already have this expertise; you don't need their recipes. However, the chef across the street may appreciate the recipes. Although you may be underwhelmed by the free recipes, he or she may view them as a value enhancement.

We suppose one of the main things to keep in mind about vendor selection is that each one brings something different to the table. It is your job to find the ones that bring what you need. It's a never-ending process. A day doesn't go by when you are either buying something, thinking about buying something, or searching for that elusive perfect purveyor. And guess what? A day doesn't go by when a vendor doesn't change its combination of qualities, support functions, and AP prices. Go to the blackboard and write 100 times:

> *Vendor selection is where my cost of sales begins. I will not get lazy. I will not get too comfortable with my vendors. I will always be looking to increase the value of what I buy.*

MOST IMPORTANT VENDOR-SELECTION CRITERIA

What are the most important selection factors? If you had to pick only one or two, what would it (they) be?

Like almost every important detail in the foodservice business, there are no right or wrong answers, just different ones. You have to judge for yourself the best way to go. And to help you with that process, we'd like to share with you what seems to be the most common approach.

Generally, most buyers are interested primarily in obtaining the product quality they need. Vendors must be able to consistently provide the quality desired, or else you can't deal with them.

Supplier services are usually a close second to product quality. Dependability is especially critical. Purveyors must ensure that buyers receive what they need when they need it. Stockouts and back orders are bad news.

The AP price tends to trail product quality and supplier services in most buyer surveys. This doesn't mean that buyers are unconcerned with product costs. However, the typical buyer will not go with the lowest AP price if it means sacrificing more important considerations.

It would appear that most buyers in our business follow the vendor selection process that Walt Disney World food services adopted some time ago. When selecting its purveyors, Disney is concerned with product quality, supplier services, whether the vendor is large enough to handle the account, and AP prices (Stephen M. Fjellman, *Vinyl Leaves: Walt Disney World and America* [San Francisco: Westview Press, 1992], p. 390).

Regardless of the number and type of vendor-selection criteria employed, the common thread running through them is one of consistency, dependability, loyalty, and trust. If purveyors can render consistent value, chances are you and many other chefs will be loyal customers (at least until a better deal comes along).

APPLY WHAT YOU'VE LEARNED

You have just been hired as the kitchen manager at a new, independently owned restaurant. The menu is set, you have a fully qualified staff, and it is a month before opening. The owners have provided you with a list of ten supplier options, from which you must pick three. They tell you first to ask about ordering procedures. What questions will you ask when the suppliers call tomorrow morning to solicit your business?

DISCUSSION QUESTIONS

1. What are some ways you think vendor selection might affect your cost of sales?

2. How might vendor selection change in a franchise or national chain concept, as opposed to an independent restaurant?

3. What are some things you can find out about vendors through references?

4. How important is compatibility with the vendor to a chef? Do you think how much you get along with a purveyor is very important personally, or not that important?

5. What are some of the advantages and disadvantages of dealing with a large purveyor instead of a small one?

6. Why might a restaurant want a vendor that is close by?

7. What is *will-call* buying?

8. How important do you think control over the delivery schedule is to your F & B operation or one you have previously worked at? Why?

9. How can storage availability help the operation when it comes to purchasing?

10. What are some of the pros and cons of having more or less face-to-face and telephone contact with a vendor, as opposed to online contact?

11. What is reciprocal buying? What can buyers expect from this type of relationship? Explain it in your own words, and give an example.

12. What are trade-outs? Give an example.

13. What types of credit terms do you think you might need if you opened your own restaurant? What problems would you incur if you couldn't pay your suppliers in a timely manner?

14. How could cost-plus purchasing affect a foodservice operation?

15. What do people mean when they say sole-source procurement, prime-vendor procurement, preferred provider procurement, or single-source procurement?

16. What advantages and disadvantages does a standing order offer to F & B operations?

17. What is perceived value? Briefly describe, in a sentence or two, how it relates to quality.

18. What are AP price and EP cost? Which do you think is more important to monitor?

4

PURCHASE
ORDERS

How Much Stuff
Should I Buy?

CHAPTER OUTLINE

- YIELD TESTS
- SALES FORECASTING
- ORDER SIZE
- ADJUSTMENTS TO ORDER SIZES

LEARNING OBJECTIVES

☑ Discuss the consequences of over- and underordering.

☑ Calculate acceptable order sizes, EP weight, and edible product yield.

☑ Examine and diagnose causes of product loss.

☑ Prepare sales forecasts needed to enhance the accuracy of purchasing decisions.

Calculating the appropriate amount of product to order is much easier said than done. We tend to stress out over this task. While we don't want to overorder, we eventually tend to focus on *not* running out of food and beverage. We do not want to approach the table and tell the guest we are out of this and that. In our opinion, **stockouts**—shortages—should be rigorously avoided. However, even though we want to avoid running out, if it occasionally happens, and if we have acceptable options to suggest, the guest may not be very disappointed.

The trick to calculating the correct order size is to make an attempt to balance the cost of having inventory sitting on your shelves (usually referred to as the **carrying cost** or **storage cost**) with the cost of running out of things and irritating guests (usually referred to as the **stockout cost**).

There are a gazillion inventory management computer programs out there that can help you balance these two costs. They help you forecast your sales and simultaneously give you a pretty good idea of how much product you need to buy in order to handle the expected amount of business. A large, multiunit restaurant company that provides this type of corporate support is a huge advantage, a great tool that helps you manage your inventories. However, even with a healthy dose of this type of technology, someone still has to come up with the data the computer programs need to make these calculations. That's where you come in.

If you want to fine-tune your order sizes so that they are as close as possible to the ideal ones, you have a lot of work to do. Whether you have access to the most sophisticated technology in the world, or you're like most of us plodding along with a run-of-the-mill PC, you still need to complete three primary tasks in order to come up with acceptable order sizes:

1. *Conduct a yield test.* Calculate the expected amount of product you can get from each food item you purchase.

2. *Forecast sales.* Forecast the expected amount of business between deliveries.

3. *Determine order size.* Calculate the amount of as-purchased (AP) product needed.

YIELD TESTS

If you ask culinary students to name one of the things they didn't like about their formal studies, many of them will mention **yield tests.** They're right up there with doing your taxes. But they are absolutely, positively necessary if you ever hope to control your order sizes as well as the total inventory you have on hand.

Before proceeding with the yield test, you need to buy the product you are considering for your operation. Better yet, get two or three free samples from the purveyor. If that's too greedy for you, ask for one free sample and buy the others. You need more than one sample because a yield test for each product you buy should be done at least twice, maybe more, to verify the results.

Next step: Calculate the item's **as-purchased (AP) weight.** For most products it is easy, but that is not true for everything, especially for fresh meats, fish, and poultry. For instance, if you are using a large primal cut of beef as a roast beef entrée, it will have a particular weight when you receive the shipment. However, after you let it sit around in the walk-in for a day or so, it can lose quite a bit of weight due to moisture loss. In fact, when you order a product like this and stipulate a certain weight, some purveyors will want you to give them a **shrink allowance**—that is, while it may weigh what you want at the purveyor's warehouse, he or she wants to know how much shrink you'll allow because it may weigh a little less by the time it gets to your restaurant. One way to minimize the shrink effect is to specify that these types of items be **Cryovac-packed (wet-packed)**—that is, packed in shrink-wrap material—as this will help to prevent moisture loss. **Ice pack, chill-pack,** and frozen preservation methods can also help prevent moisture loss. Unfortunately, though, you can't assume these options are available for everything you purchase. Furthermore, you may not want to buy products packed this way because they may not have the culinary quality you prefer.

Next, you need to put the product through the exact production and service procedures you will be using in your restaurant. While doing this, you will want to calculate very carefully how much waste you incur, which, when subtracted from the AP weight, will give you the **edible-portion (EP) weight** (sometimes referred to as the **usable weight** or **servable weight**). This will take a bit of time because you should do the test more than once and average the results. This will increase the accuracy of your numbers.

Unless you purchase **convenience foods** that need no further handling, you will have some product loss. It's only a question of how much it's going to be. Many things cause product loss. Here are five of the most typical ones to watch for:

1. *Mise en place.* During this pre-preparation stage you will typically have cutting and trimming loss, most of it unavoidable.

2. *Production loss.* If you cook an item you will usually have shrinkage to account for. There can be considerable shrinkage with roasted foods, especially if you cook something well-done. You may also have some trimming to do once the product is cooked. For instance, a roast beef might have to have some of the fat removed after cooking. You might also have to discard the end cuts. And there might be some unusable portions, such as broken pieces, that cannot be served. For some products, such as beverages, there will also be spillage and overpouring to account for.

3. *Pilferage.* There will be some eating and drinking on the job no matter how vigilant you are. You have to do your best to keep it down; however, you need to be realistic and

plan for this. Don't think that pilferage happens only at the bar. It happens everywhere in your restaurant. As the late, great Joe Baum, developer of the Windows on the World restaurant, once remarked, the staff has to eat, too.

4. *Unanticipated mistakes.* Like pilferage, something wrong is going to happen, especially when you are super busy. If you have long-term, highly skilled employees working for you, this may be a minor issue. But if you have a lot of labor turnover, and/or a lot of interns on your staff, you are going to have more product handling problems. You will have more finished menu items that the expeditor will refuse to send out. And you will have more guests sending things back.

5. *Style of service.* If you preplate everything in the kitchen, this issue should not concern you. But if you have offerings such as all-you-can-eat items on the menu, food bars in the dining room, self-serve soda pop machines, unlimited refills, and so on, you need to spend some time determining the average portion size of these products. For example, the big hotel/casinos in Las Vegas may analyze over a two-week period the amount of food inventory used at the buffets during that time. They will then divide it by the number of total customers served during that period. This gives them an average portion size that, while not as accurate as you'd like, is about as good as it gets.

Once you calculate the total expected product loss, your next step is to subtract it from the AP weight. The result will be the EP weight. You then divide the EP weight by the AP weight, and multiply by 100, to get the **edible yield percentage** for that product. Once you have the edible (or *servable* or *usable*) yield percentage, you can easily compute the amount of AP weight you need to purchase in order to serve a specific number of guests.

The most accurate method of determining the edible yield percentage is to conduct your own yield tests. This is the only way you can ensure that you take into account everything that's relevant to your particular restaurant's operating procedures. Calculating edible yield percentages for all the different foods and beverages you use will be time and labor intensive. One way to speed up the calculations is to rely on purveyors' estimates of edible yield percentages. We don't usually recommend that option because purveyors might unknowingly overstate the percentages, since their analyses are typically done in a lab setting and not in the typical restaurant kitchen and bar. We suppose, though, that you can start with them and adjust them to fit your operation.

A better option is to pick up two excellent books that contain edible yield percentages for just about every product you can think of. The Lynch title, *The Book of Yields,* and the Schmidt reference book, *Chef's Book of Formulas, Yields, and Sizes,* should be on your bookshelf. These chefs have spent years calculating portion sizes and edible yield percentages just to make our lives a little easier.

An alternative to calculating the edible yield percentage for each item is to compute the number of expected servings in a unit of product. This can't be done for everything, but is possible when you purchase a lot of large, raw, whole foods, such as **primal cuts** of meat, that you intend to process in your kitchen. (It's also possible when you buy a lot of bottled beverages.) For instance, if you consistently purchase the same quality and size of standing rib roast, sooner or later you will learn how many servings each roast will give you. If, say, you note that you always get about 20 retail cuts per roast, then your order size will be one roast for every 20 guests you think will order this menu item.

Yield testing gets more tricky and more time-consuming when you like to shop around a lot. You have to perform a new test before you change vendors. Or, if you compare two or three vendors' products, you may have to use different edible yield percentages for each one. But when you shop around you incur a lot of extra work all the way down the line, from purchasing, to receiving, to bill paying, and so forth. You have to work harder to save money. Nobody's going to give it to you.

SALES FORECASTING

Before giving purchase orders to your vendors, you need to forecast how much product you'll need to last between regularly scheduled deliveries. Generally, you have two main types of business: the regular restaurant sales, such as dine-in, take-out, and delivery business, and the catering volume.

1. *Regular sales.* The best way to estimate these needs is to rely on recent history taken from your **Point-of-Sale** POS system. The computer tracks past sales and calculates a

menu mix percentage (also referred to as a **popularity index**) for each menu item you serve. Menu mix percentage is calculated as follows:

$$\text{Menu mix percentage} = \frac{\textbf{Number of specific menu item served}}{\textbf{Number of total meals served}}$$

For instance, if you normally sell 1,000 meals per day, and on average 50 persons purchase the seafood special entrée, the menu mix percentage for this menu item is 5 percent (50 ÷ 1,000 = 0.05 = 5 percent). That percentage can be used to predict future sales of the seafood special. If, for example, you anticipate serving 10,000 meals next week, you should plan to have on hand enough food to prepare 500 seafood specials (10,000 × .05 = 500). If you anticipate any unusual business trends next week—say, for instance, there will be unseasonably bitter cold weather—you may want to reduce your estimate a little.

2. *Catering sales.* These sales should be easy to estimate because you typically book them weeks or months in advance. It's merely necessary to add up what you need, inflate it a little so that you don't run out, and prepare the purchase order. The hassle in catering is determining the extra amount of food and beverage to purchase so that you can handle any excess over the guaranteed number of guests. If the foods and beverages you're serving to a private party are off your regular menus, this isn't too much of a headache because you will be able to get more from the main kitchen and bar to take care of any extra guests who show up unannounced. But if the private party is having products you don't normally carry in inventory, you will have to order an extra amount, even though it may go to waste, just to be on the safe side. If the party's guarantee is 100 guests or less, you should order 10 percent more; if the guarantee ranges from 100 to 1,000 guests, order 5 percent more; and if the guarantee exceeds 1,000 guests, order 3 percent more. Our advice to you is: Don't ever run out. It's one of the worst things that can happen. The function host will never hear the end of it. And neither will you

PURCHASING'S LINK TO SERVICE

Buyers have to ensure that the service staff has enough supplies to perform its work. All marketing and promotional campaigns typically rely on purchasing to procure the products needed to ensure guest satisfaction. In addition, the chef must clearly communicate menu changes to everyone in the restaurant.

ORDER SIZE

There is a formula to calculate a product's order size:

$$\textbf{AP amount to order} = \frac{\textbf{EP amount needed}}{\textbf{Edible yield percentage}}$$

Let's use the example of broccoli. If you buy whole broccoli, but cut it into florets for service, you trim off a lot of stems and leaves in the process. The amount cut off would be the loss, and the amount remaining would be the edible portion. If you begin with one AP pound of broccoli and have 12 ounces left over after trimming, the edible yield percentage will be 75 percent (12 ounces (EP) ÷ 16 ounces (AP) = 0.75 = 75%).

Here's how to use the edible yield percentage to calculate the order size. Suppose a banquet chef wants to serve a 4-ounce (EP) portion of broccoli florets as a side vegetable to 600 guests. Therefore, she needs 4 ounces × 600, or 2,400 (EP) ounces of florets. The AP amount to purchase is equal to the EP amount (2,400 ounces) divided by the edible yield percentage (75%, or 0.75), or 3,200 (AP) ounces. Converting the 3,200 ounces to pounds, she needs to order at least 200 (AP) pounds of whole broccoli. We would recommend ordering a bit more just to be safe.

Here's another example. A chef serves a great hot turkey sandwich using turkey roasted fresh daily. It's been determined that a 10-pound (AP) fresh, boneless, turkey breast yields 9 pounds (EP), the amount left over after cooking, removing the skin, and slicing it. The standard portion size of turkey is 6 ounces (EP). If you expect that every day 200 hungry guests will order the hot turkey sandwich, how many raw turkey breasts should you order each day?

1. 9 pounds (EP) ÷ 10 pounds (AP) = 0.90, or 90% edible yield percentage

2. 6 ounces × 200 guests = 1,200 ounces (EP)

3. 1,200 ounces ÷ 0.90 = 1,333 ounces (AP)

4. 1,333 ounces ÷ 16 ounces per pound = 83 pounds (AP)

If the turkey breasts consistently weigh 10 pounds apiece (AP), then you have to decide whether to order eight or nine of them. Eight is OK if you don't care if you run out of product or have a little left over from the day before that can be used as backup. Alternately, you could order nine one day and eight the next; and if you have leftovers piling up, they could be used for turkey soup once in a while. We would play it safe and order nine turkey breasts every day. But by playing it safe, over the long run the food cost may increase slightly because you can't always trust that the leftover turkey will be good enough to serve the next day. Nor can you always find a use for the leftovers. Furthermore, the extra inventory oftentimes leads your staff to think that if there is so much of it around, why not give a little more than 6 ounces (EP) to each guest? When a lot of stuff is lying around, there's a tendency to get careless and wasteful.

How about another example. Let's say that there is a party planned for tomorrow night for 100 guests, and that the main entrée will be roast beef. You want to serve a 6-ounce portion (EP). If the roast beef you typically purchase has an edible yield percentage of 75 percent, how many AP pounds of roast should you order?

1. Divide serving size by edible yield percentage. This will tell you how much AP product you need per serving.
6 ounces (EP) ÷ 0.75 = 8 ounces (AP).

2. Divide 16 ounces by the amount of AP product needed per serving. This will tell you the number of edible servings you can get from one AP pound of roast beef.
16 ounces ÷ 8 ounces (AP) = 2 servings.

3. Divide the number of guests by the number of edible servings per AP pound. This will give you the amount of AP roast beef you need to order.
110 servings ÷ 2 = 55 pounds (AP).

Notice that we used 110 guests (10 percent safety factor). This is the rule of thumb we follow for 100 or fewer guests (see previous catering sales forecast discussion). You know by now the word *stockout* is not in our vocabulary. We always buy more than we need. We know we'll waste some of it. We know that **pilferage** (minor theft) will increase. And so forth. That is why when we calculate recipe costs and menu prices, we always bump them up a bit to account for these things. In the long run, it really doesn't cost you that much more; plus, a catering event is typically priced sky high to begin with. The biggest problem you'll have is the fact that it is almost impossible to order exactly 55 pounds (AP) of roast beef. For these kinds of products, you can't specify an exact weight; you have to go along with something called the **catch weight.** For instance, if your purveyor sells this product by the case, the total weight of the case will vary. You have to try to get the case that's closest to your requirement, but that isn't easy. You will most likely have to order more than 55 pounds in this example. It's sort of like going to the supermarket meat counter and rifling through the prepackaged meats looking for one that has the weight best suited for your needs at home that night. Oh well; thank goodness for employee meals.

Let's look at one more example, this one dealing with alcoholic beverages. Let's assume that you wish to purchase a wine for your restaurant that will be sold by the glass. The serving size is 5 servable ounces. According to past history, you estimate that you can sell only about 90 percent of the bottle; the other 10 percent is lost to spillage, overpouring, pilferage, sediment in the bottle, and so on. You also estimate that you will sell about 100 glasses of this wine each day. The wine you want to buy comes in a 750 ml bottle. The question, then, is: How many bottles should you order, say, for one week?

1. Divide the serving size by the servable yield percentage. This will tell you how much AP wine you need per serving. 5 servable ounces ÷ 0.90 = 5.5 ounces (AP).

2. Divide the AP amount of wine in a 750 ml bottle by the amount of AP wine needed for one serving. This will tell you how many servings you can obtain per bottle. 25.4 ounces (AP) ÷ 5.5 ounces (AP) = 4.6 drinks per bottle. (Note that there are 25.4 ounces in a 750 ml bottle of wine.)

3. Divide the total number of servings needed per week by the number of drinks you can get from each bottle. This will tell you how many bottles you must order.

700 servings per week $\div$ 4.6 = 152.2 bottles, rounded to 153 bottles. Since this type of item normally comes packed 12 bottles per case, you will need to order 13 cases (156 bottles). But since this product is not as perishable as most foods, it's not much of a burden to have a little extra on hand. You just have to make sure that you rotate your stock correctly.

ADJUSTMENTS TO ORDER SIZES

These order size examples assume you don't have any stock on hand, that your refrigerators, freezers, and stock rooms are empty. But this is not normal. Consequently, when you compute your order sizes, you have to take a physical inventory (count) before you make your final calculation. The bulk of this type of work is usually done on Monday mornings, when your inventories are typically at their lowest levels, just prior to preparing your purchase orders for the week. (Well, let's just say that ideally we do most of this only on Monday morning.) If you have anything on hand, you would reduce your order sizes, assuming that the old inventory is good enough to serve.

The primary adjustment we've already mentioned—how much extra stuff should you buy to be on the safe side—bears repeating. *We* don't mind overordering a little because, being primarily a catering facility at a college, we can jack up the prices a little to account for it. It's easy for us because we build every party from scratch; there are no preprinted menus. But this is not the case in a typical restaurant. Somebody's going to have to decide how many stockouts are too many. Our guess is, that somebody is you.

APPLY WHAT YOU'VE LEARNED

You're working on a purchase order for a special menu that will run the week of Valentine's Day. The menu is a six-course *prix fixe* that features a wine paired with each course. The serving size of each wine for the six-course meal is as follows:

Champagne: 3 ounces

Muscadet: 4 ounces

Chardonnay: 4 ounces

Champagne: 4 ounces

Cabernet: 4 ounces

Icewine: 2 ounces

Your bar manager tells you that there is a 95 percent yield on wines in the restaurant, due mainly to unavoidable spillage and overpouring. The special menu is estimated to attract a total of 1,200 covers during the week. All wines come in 750 ml bottles, with the exception of the icewine, which comes in 375 ml bottles. How many bottles of each wine should you order for the week?

DISCUSSION QUESTIONS

1. What are the consequences of over- and underordering?

2. Give an example of how underordering can result in lower profits.

3. What three things need to be done to compute acceptable order sizes?

4. What is a shrink allowance? Why do some purveyors want it?

5. What is EP weight? How is it calculated?

6. What things typically cause product loss?

7. What is the most accurate method of determining the edible yield percentage? Why? What are some alternate methods?

8. What are some ways to forecast sales?

9. What is an appropriate formula to use in order to calculate an order size?

10. What do we mean when we say *catch weight*?

5

PURCHASE
PRICES

How Do I Get the Best Deal?

CHAPTER OUTLINE

- VALUE REVISITED
- REDUCING COSTS

LEARNING OBJECTIVES

☑ Discuss the concept of value and its dimensions.

☑ Understand the relationship among AP price, EP cost, and value.

☑ Cost out standardized recipes.

☑ Compare the AP prices and EP costs from multiple vendors.

☑ Suggest a variety of methods to increase overall value.

☑ Suggest a variety of ways to reduce AP prices.

Theoretically, the best deal represents the best overall value. In reality, we want the lowest possible AP price, because that is the one that most of the time (not all of the time) will give us what we are really after: the lowest possible edible (servable or usable) portion (EP) cost. At its fundamental level, value is heavily influenced by the EP costs. Your goal, then, is to minimize them.

VALUE REVISITED

However, as mentioned earlier in this book, value has many other dimensions. The quality of products you buy is another major influence on value. Generally speaking, the higher the quality, the more you have to pay for the item. But since quality is based primarily on appearance factors, you should not ignore things that don't look so nice because they are wholesome products that may fit your needs. Your job is not to go after the highest value for the lowest AP price, but to make sure you know the appropriate quality needed for your intended use. Your **quality control** focus, then, must be on determining what the quality should be, no more and no less, and figuring out how to ensure that you receive it every time you order it for the best possible AP price. The same thing can be said about supplier services. Focus on what you absolutely have to have, not on what you don't need. It's easy to get swayed by vendors who want to charge you just "pennies more" for a big bump up in quality. If you don't need a Cadillac, don't buy it. Buy only what you need.

There is a caveat, however: It may be impossible to **cherry-pick** your purveyors. If you want to do business with a certain vendor, it may require you to adjust to his or her method of operation. For instance, if you want to pick up your orders at the vendor's warehouse, the vendor may say no. Alternately, a vendor may allow you to pick up your own orders, but if you want a discount for providing your own delivery, you may be out of luck. The AP price may be the same no matter who does the delivering.

We could go on and on about value. Entire books have been devoted to this elusive subject. Our advice: If you know exactly, positively, beyond a shadow of a doubt, what you need, have a good head for numbers, and are not overly influenced by the sales reps banging on your back door, you can increase your overall value by focusing on reducing the AP prices you have to pay.

■ SPECIFICATIONS REVISITED

The first step, then, when going after the best possible deal is to know the intended use of each product you buy. This is a big reason why specifications are so important. If you don't have a firm grasp of your needs, you can easily fall victim to all sorts of sales presentations. If you surrender the driver's seat to your vendors, they will gladly take you for a ride.

■ STANDARD RECIPES REVISITED

Standard recipes are just as critical as specifications. The two work hand in hand. When you first open your restaurant, usually you develop the recipes before the specifications. But as you go on, you tend to work on them simultaneously.

You need to cost out each standard recipe. There are several reasons to do this, but the one most pertinent to this discussion is that it allows you to tell at a glance if there are any expensive ingredients that should be analyzed for potential cost savings. The recipes should be set up in such a way that they contain the AP amount of each ingredient needed. Once you have the correct AP amount for each one, you can multiply the amount by that ingredient's AP price to determine the total cost for that ingredient. Add up the cost of all the ingredients in the recipe, divide it by the number of servings the recipe makes, and you have the **standard** (i.e., expected) **cost** for one portion. There are a few additional twists to recipe costing (e.g., you may want to bump up the portion cost a little in order to account for things like bread, butter, and other condiments on the table or on the self-serve bars), but this procedure will get you started in the right direction.

Now you're going to hate us. We can't leave this discussion of recipe costing without noting that you cannot cost out only one version of a recipe. You need to cost out as many as there are potential vendors for the items used in that recipe. For instance, if you have a killer recipe for meat loaf, you need to cost it out using the edible yield percentages of each vendor who sells, or could sell, meat to you. If you like to shop around a lot, it is absolutely, no doubt about it, necessary to use the correct **yield percentages.** If you don't, you will fall into the trap of assuming that the meat you buy from Vendor A has the same yield as the one purchased from Vendor B. Even if it's the same quality, we can almost guarantee that the edible yield will be different. Do not, we repeat, do not jump to another vendor until you do a yield test. Don't get lazy.

If you've paid attention to your computer instructors, you can easily set up different versions of the same recipe on a spreadsheet, such as Excel. Or you can purchase one of the many recipe-costing programs available, most of which are not very expensive. When you spot a big-enough AP price variation among purveyors, you can then swoop down and order from the vendor who is truly less expensive. You will know who gives you the better deal because you will know exactly what to expect. You can quickly run the numbers with the updated AP prices before preparing the purchase order.

If you don't have time or the interest to cost out a lot of recipes, you can cheat a little by tracking only the most expensive ingredients used in your kitchen. The average restaurant kitchen has about 600 to 800 ingredients in stock, but typically only about 20 to 25 of them account for almost 80 percent of your total food purchases. You could habitually check the AP prices of these ingredients on a regular basis and simultaneously convert each AP price to its EP cost.

Let's say that you use a lot of fresh beef brisket in your operation. And let's further assume that you can get similar brisket from three different vendors. If you take the time to calculate the edible yield (EP) percentage of each vendor's brisket you can easily determine which one has the better deal.

Let's assume that Vendor A sells the brisket for $3.79 per pound, Vendor B asks $4.25 per pound, and Vendor C, $4.15. Vendor A's yield percentage is 75 percent, B's is 90 percent, and C's is 82 percent. All other things being equal, or similar (things like delivery schedule, bill-paying procedures, etc.), which vendor offers the best value?

Here's the formula that answers this question:

$$\frac{\textbf{AP price per unit}}{\textbf{Edible yield percentage}} = \textbf{EP cost per unit}$$

Vendor A: $3.79 ÷ 0.75 = $5.05 (EP) cost per pound
Vendor B: $4.25 ÷ 0.90 = $4.72 (EP) cost per pound
Vendor C: $4.15 ÷ 0.82 = $5.06 (EP) cost per pound

If you considered only the AP price per pound, you would go straight for Vendor A's product. However, it is much more expensive in the long run. Your concern should be on the EP cost per unit instead of the AP price per unit. As we've mentioned elsewhere in this text, you have to pay very close attention to the yield variations when you buy foods. And to do that, you need to—you guessed it—perform yield tests regularly. You don't care what the AP price is; your focus needs to be on the EP cost. Therefore, Vendor B looks like the best bet, for now. Tomorrow is another day.

If you have only enough time to track the 25 most expensive ingredients in your kitchen, you have to be willing to let the other ones slide. You certainly can't let the quality slide, but if you work under severe time constraints, you must be willing to forfeit some cost accuracy. In some cases you have to make that tradeoff. Unless you work in a large organization that has a good deal of accounting support, you may not have the luxury of spending much of your valuable time chasing a few nickels. It may not be cost-effective in the long run.

Another strategy you can employ to reduce the need to continually calculate hundreds of edible yield percentages is to buy as many products as possible that almost guarantee a 100 percent yield. There

---

↕ PURCHASING'S LINK TO THE PLANNING PROCESS

Most long-term and short-term plans eventually require someone to spend some money. Buyers can provide historical data and expense estimates in addition to being the ones who actually go out and spend the money.

---

are many convenience foods that you can purchase. In our opinion, the AP prices of these items are exorbitant. Plus, the culinary quality for many of them is suspect. We have no problem with the many **first-generation convenience foods,** such as canned tomatoes and frozen orange juice, because they normally are not center-plate items. And they usually do not sell for a premium AP price; most of the time they are cheaper than many of their fresh counterparts. We also are OK with things like precut steaks, chops, chicken parts, and other similar items. Many of these are fresh or fresh frozen products that have been cut and trimmed at the vendor's warehouse or at the food processor's plant. Instead of buying, say, a large primal cut of beef and cutting your own steaks, you buy the steaks already cut. In some cases it is cheaper to do this because you transfer the labor and energy expense from your restaurant to some other location. Also, since you don't have to have a large production kitchen, you may save some money by renting a smaller retail site for your restaurant. We're not so sure, though, that the potential savings will offset the higher AP prices. You need to be cautious when you start adding convenience foods to your menu. Don't do it unless you're pretty sure that it is the most economical way of achieving your business objectives.

REDUCING COSTS

Cost control is the system of ensuring that actual costs are in line with **budgeted** costs, which we want to reduce as much as possible. The most productive way to reduce AP prices and to get the best possible value is to track the vendor prices for the things you buy and to shift your business toward the best ones. You have to shop around all the time; of all possible cost-saving opportunities, this is the most effective one, especially for the typical restaurant operator who isn't part of a large, multiunit restaurant company. But if you're going to play that game, you have to have a very, very good handle on the relevant edible yield percentages.

There are other ways to potentially reduce your cost of goods sold and/or other costs of doing business. Here are some ideas pertinent to the purchasing function that you might want to consider.

■ REDUCE PRODUCT QUALITY

This is a risky strategy. If you have a repeat clientele who are used to a certain quality, you should not change it. It would be disastrous. You'd be better off bumping up the menu prices a little to earn more revenue. If your clientele changes frequently, your restaurant is a place people visit for reasons other than the food, or your restaurant is located in a tourist trap, you might be able to get away with this option. But even then, it's a dicey situation. People today know a lot about food; many of them seldom eat at home, and even then they may eat take-out food. It's not easy to fool them. Again, a little menu price increase for some items may be the better option. Be very careful before you alter your quality standards.

■ REDUCE PORTION SIZE

This is a better alternative than reducing product quality. If you are in a very competitive environment, a slight decrease for some menu items can be just what the doctor ordered. For instance, we once saved quite a few pennies by reducing the coffee creamers to $\frac{3}{8}$ ounce from $\frac{1}{2}$ ounce. The only problem was, the savings didn't last very long. After a while, some guests started using $1\frac{1}{2}$ to 2 creamers, where before they used only one. Oh well, back to the drawing board.

We can think of a lot of ways to reduce portion sizes without making the guests upset. We're certain you can, too. An ounce here, a $\frac{1}{2}$ ounce there, might be invisible to all but the most discerning guest, especially if you adjust for visual effect by using the proper plateware. But it can have a huge impact on your bottom line. As always, though, be careful before going down this road. It can backfire on you. Remember the coffee creamer example.

▣ USE SUBSTITUTE PRODUCTS

Here is where your culinary training can really pay off. Your ability to reshuffle ingredients, use different ingredients, and use by-products from other menu items to come up with a winning menu item is priceless. Guests will enjoy the variety, and you will enjoy the added profits.

To take full advantage of this option you must be willing to learn something new every day. You have to look at the magazines, talk to other chefs, track consumer trends, and so on. You also have to understand thoroughly what kinds of substitutes will work to your advantage. The idea is to substitute something less expensive for something more expensive, not the other way around. A recipe that saves on meat cost, but needs expensive spices, flavorings, and/or a tenderization procedure to make it palatable, may not work.

A good example is something like flank steak. Here's an item that can be used for several dishes. Yet, depending on the cut and the degree of processing you buy, it can be very expensive. But you may be able to adapt its cousin, the skirt steak, to some of your recipes without any noticeable drop in quality or in customer acceptance. It takes a super chef to be able to pull that off. You probably won't get a TV show for that type of low-profile, below-the-radar skill, but your bank account might be healthier than some of the celebrity chefs who grace the food networks.

Substitution is a little trick that the big institutional feeders like to use. For instance, the foodservice contractors that manage school and college food operations typically have several recipes for the same menu items stored in a gigantic database. It's nothing for them to have, for instance, a dozen or so recipes for baked macaroni and cheese, each one having similar culinary quality. Usually, someone at the company headquarters stays on top of AP prices for the more expensive ingredients, such as cheese. When these prices change a little, given the huge volume the company does, a few pennies saved here and there will quickly add up. If, say, the AP price of medium cheddar drops, goodbye sharp cheddar, hello medium.

You probably have already figured out that the bar manager doesn't have the same options you do when it comes to beverage service. Beverage alcohol is a very standardized, tightly controlled, exclusively distributed product that is not subject to the type of spoilage and inconsistent quality you incur with some foods. Less options means less opportunity to finagle recipes in order to save a buck or two.

People ask us all the time: What are the primary characteristics employers look for when hiring chefs? That's easy. It's the culinary skill. Let's face it, no one comes to your restaurant because you have the best purchasing system. If the chef can't work with all sorts of ingredients to capitalize on price swings, you won't be able to take advantage of a good way to save money, and you might miss out on a creative combination of leftovers and trimmings from other foods that customers can't get enough of.

But just because you can take a mystery basket of ingredients and create a fantastic meal doesn't mean that the ingredients in the basket are the most cost-effective ones. These days you have to be a great chef and a great businessperson (or have one working alongside you) if you want to survive. There are other ways to save money, that's true. But it's much easier to take an accomplished chef and teach him or her the necessary business skills than it is to turn a bean counter into a great chef.

■ MINIMIZE THE USE OF CONVENIENCE FOODS

We don't mind repeating ourselves: Be careful with convenience foods. They are horribly expensive. And we are skeptical of the claim that they reduce your labor costs significantly. They probably do, in some cases. But whether the labor cost reduction offsets the food cost increase is not clear.

We don't want to be overly critical of convenience foods, because there are other good reasons to use them. They enhance your quality control efforts considerably. Since they require minimal handling, food safety is much easier to maintain. They are a good choice if you are in a tight labor market where it is difficult to find the quality of labor you need to make things from scratch. And they are useful if your kitchen is the size of a postage stamp. But in the long run, you're going to pay dearly for these advantages.

Not too long ago, one of us was visiting someone in the main production kitchen of one of the large hotel/casino properties in southern Nevada. This place is so big that the executive chef has to use a golf cart to get around to all the kitchens and service corridors. Heck, you could easily park a 707 airplane in its dry storage area and not take up all the space.

Anyway, while hanging out, he noticed that a prep cook was preparing chicken rice soup. She filled up a steam kettle with water, added a large blob of Minor's chicken base, a box of rice, a few cans of tomatoes, some chopped vegetables, and a box of frozen, cooked, pulled chicken. Slammed the lid down. Set the timer. Walked away. Think about it. This place is loaded with employees and has the best and latest, most modern kitchen equipment, but somewhere along the line someone got the idea that they could make something like chicken rice soup easier and cheaper by using almost all convenience foods. While not being surprised that some convenience products, like chicken base, were used, it seemed a bit much to purchase frozen, cooked, pulled chicken. As far as we're concerned, the price of that box alone could have been used to make a river of chicken rice soup from scratch.

This brings to mind another cute story noted in *Kitchen Confidential*. It seems that one of the first things the author, Chef Anthony Bourdain, checks when he shows up at his restaurant in the morning is the previous day's sales of frites. Since they are made from scratch, the more sold, the better it is for his food cost. Even though it takes a full-time employee to prepare an item with a food cost of about 5 percent, we don't think he'd make that comment if he was buying a frozen product. Chances are, he wouldn't save a full-time employee even if he used a convenience potato product.

We think one of the main driving forces causing people to use a lot of convenience foods is the desire to offer such gigantic menus. For instance, the hotel/casino property just described offers hundreds of items on its buffets. It's gotten to the point where it's almost impossible to prepare everything from scratch, let alone preserve its quality and maintain product safety, if you offer so much. The selection is so huge that it seems necessary to rely more and more on convenience products. The same thing is happening in many restaurants throughout the country.

ONE-STOP SHOPPING

Some chefs prefer doing business with only a few purveyors. The fewer the better. This is ironic, because it will almost guarantee that your food cost will increase. However, you can expect your administrative costs to decrease. For instance, when you put in fewer orders and deal with fewer vendors, you have less paperwork, fewer deliveries, and less opportunity for error. Plus, since your purchase orders are typically much larger than if you shopped all over town, you may gain a price break from the preferred provider—though getting a price break on a product that's overpriced to begin with is hardly a bargain.

In some cases, one-stop shopping may be a good strategy in the long run. It might be the most cost-effective one. However, when you use a one-stop shopping strategy you are essentially buying convenience. And that may cost you, much the same as the premium you pay for convenience foods. To us, it's too high of a price to pay. If you plan it carefully, you can get a lot of shopping done in a short time. A few more phone calls, a little more time in front of the computer, a few more minutes on the receiving dock—these things can translate into sizable savings. In our view, it's worth the extra effort.

■ TRADE-OUTS

Trade-outs (another term for bartering) reduce your out-of-pocket expenses. It is a lot cheaper to pay a $1,000 invoice with $1,000 (retail value) worth of food and drinks. There is a limit to how much you can save, though, because not many vendors will participate. Plus, if you join a barter group, you will have to pay either a one-time enrollment fee or a fee for each transaction (as much as 10 percent of the transaction).

It seems to us that trade-outs work well when they are done directly, between you and someone else, without having to pay an intermediary. The fact that many vendors don't like to participate in these things usually means that it's difficult to work this subject into a discussion; it's hard to make a good match. You have to luck out in order to fall into one of these deals.

■ PROVIDE YOUR OWN SUPPORT FUNCTIONS

This is essentially what you do when you purchase directly from a **primary source,** such as a major manufacturer or farmer. For instance, instead of buying an ounce scale from the local restaurant supply house you go on the Internet, locate the manufacturer, and order the scale. You bypass the local vendor and perhaps realize a lower overall price for the product.

Direct buying may or may not work out for you. On the one hand, you might avoid the **sales tax** on the transaction. And you might be able to find promotional coupons on the manufacturer's Web site that you can use to further reduce the price. Plus, you can save the markup added by the local vendors who, in the case of something like an ounce scale, essentially just buy it from the manufacturer, add a markup, and sell it to you. On the other hand, you have to pay the shipping and handling costs, and they're not cheap; the local vendor's markup may be much less. Sometimes we think the companies make more money from shipping and handling than they do off the products they're selling.

When you buy direct, you also own the product once it leaves the manufacturer's back door. If you're unhappy with it, you have to go through all kinds of aggravation to return it and to resolve the problem. You usually need to pay for the stuff up front. Back orders are fairly common. And the lead time is usually much longer than if you buy locally.

We are not big fans of direct buying. We like to see it before we buy it. We're not above checking it out now and again, say for generic things like mops where the odds are good that the items will be OK when they arrive. But it's tough to do all the little things that the local vendors can do to help you.

If you're part of a large, multiunit restaurant company, direct buying will work very well because the central purchasing office will go out and piece together the support functions you absolutely have to have; they're big enough and have sufficient purchasing power to make this happen. But if you're the typical restaurant operation it's hard to handle your own deliveries, returns and allowances, and so on. You also give up the little bit of advice and gossip that the sales reps dish out. And you usually can't get any free samples of new products. You're on your own. Our guess is that you can't save enough to make this worthwhile unless you're a big operator.

CO-OP PURCHASING

A purchasing co-op is a group of buyers, each representing a different restaurant operation, who pool their individual small orders. It is the banding together of several small operators in order to consolidate their buying power. It is expected that the one large order would qualify for a lower AP price.

If you are part of a large, multiunit restaurant company, you already have **co-op buying** in place. The central purchasing office has already done all the work needed to ensure that you can get what you need for the lowest possible AP price. But if you're the typical restaurant operator, the co-op strategy can generate a tidy savings if you know what you are doing and are willing to adjust to the program.

Restaurant folks these days are not so interested in getting together to set up their own co-op ventures. The cost and time needed to develop and administer the co-op can be sizable. They may overshadow any lower AP price that the co-op negotiates. Furthermore, if you develop your own co-op, the members have to have fairly consistent and common needs. There can't be too many exceptions.

Fortunately in this Internet age, you don't have to do this work yourself. Today there are several **buying clubs** out there whose administrators have gone through all the trouble of setting up accounts with major vendors and, for a fee, will allow you to tap into their **purchasing,** or **buying power.** For that fee you can take advantage of the club's purchasing power and also receive other subtle benefits, such as the club's willingness to share profitable ideas with its members. In effect, the buying club is an easy way for small operators to hire a highly skilled, professional purchasing executive.

Sometimes the local restaurant association or other similar associations negotiate AP prices for a few things. The association members in good standing can take advantage of these negotiated prices and usually don't have to pay a fee for the privilege. In our experience, though, these associations don't accumulate a sizable number of products and services. Plus, they usually focus on negotiating for things like insurance coverage, workers' comp, accounting and bookkeeping services, and so on. They typically don't have many food and beverage options, if any.

You should look into joining one of these buying clubs. They usually offer a wide range of options so there might be some things that you can use. It doesn't hurt to try it out. Obviously, if you can't save more than the fees charged, it's a bad idea. But you won't know that until you check it out. The best way to check it out is to examine the AP prices and support functions it offers, and then surf over to the vendors' Web sites to see what they charge. At times you will be surprised at the discrepancy between them. It's sort of like going on the Expedia or Travelocity Web sites and checking the rental car prices, then shooting over to Hertz, Dollar, and the rest of them to check their prices. Sometimes the individual vendors have better prices.

The trick to exacting maximum value from a buying club is to join one that charges you a fee only if you make a purchase through its network. That way you have the option of shopping elsewhere for the best value. You can go through the club only when there is a good deal that makes sense for you.

Like other options, the co-op can work to your advantage, but only if you use it cautiously. Take advantage of it if it saves money, but realize that you can't expect every item offered through the club's network to be the best value for you. If you join a club, make sure you don't keep using it blindly. This is what the clubs want you to do, because some items are more expensive than you realize. If you don't believe it, compare some of the product prices you find at Sam's Club or Costco to the sale items' prices for the same products in your local supermarkets.

▓ DISCOUNTS

If you're part of a large restaurant corporation, discounts have already been addressed by the central purchasing staff. The negotiated AP prices you pay usually take them into account. But if you're scratching for a living like the rest of us, you definitely have to check out every possible discount that the vendors offer. Here's a hint: They don't always offer them until you ask, those sneaky little imps.

Here is a list of a dozen typical discounts available in our industry:

1. **Quantity discount.** This is granted by the purveyor if you agree to purchase a large amount of one specific type of product.

2. **Volume discount.** This one is similar to the quantity discount. You must agree to purchase a huge volume of goods. However, you are allowed to buy more than one type of merchandise. This discount is sometimes referred to as a **blanket-order discount** or a **drop-size discount,** in that the purchase order contains a long list of several items, none of which is ordered in huge amounts. But when all of these small amounts are totaled, there is a large dollar volume that the vendor might reward with a discount.

3. **Prime-vendor discount.** This is similar to the volume discount. If you purchase most of your products from a single vendor, it might grant a discount. In our experience,

you would have to buy approximately 90 percent of your total purchases from this single vendor in order to qualify for the discount.

4. **Cash discount.** This is an award for prompt payment, for paying in advance of the delivery, or using a **cash-on-delivery (COD)** bill-paying procedure. You don't see this one as much these days. Usually, the reward for paying your bills this way is avoiding interest charges on the unpaid balance.

5. **Promotional discount.** A purveyor might grant this type of discount if you allow him or her to promote the item in your restaurant or if you personally help promote it. For instance, the promotion might involve letting restaurant customers sample the product at a reduced menu price. Alternately, some vendors, such as Coke and Pepsi, may help you pay part of your menu printing or menu sign board costs if you're willing to let them display their logos on them.

6. **Forklift discount.** You might receive a discount if you agree to unload your own shipments instead of requiring the drivers to do the unloading.

7. **User discount.** This comes into play when you use an outside contractor to install and maintain vending machines in your restaurant. Usually you can use the machines at no cost (such as a CD juke box or videogames) or at a reduced cost (such as a soft drink machine).

8. **Introductory discount.** This is a reward usually given by vendors to get you to try out new products. They may also offer to let you buy one, get one free, or some other similar discount combination.

9. **Trade-show discount.** Vendors at **trade shows** usually have demo models and/or product samples they do not want to take back to the warehouse. They would rather sell them to you at a discount. Warning: Before you whip out your credit card, make sure you know precisely what the stuff normally sells for. Don't ever assume that you're getting a good deal. Furthermore, if you're thinking about purchasing equipment like this, make sure that you understand what the delivery options are, if the guarantee remains in effect, and so forth. Don't come home with a

salad chopper that you can get at the local discount store for much less than the vendor is asking.

10. **Freight-damaged discount.** This is typically offered if you are willing to accept a floor model or an item that was damaged in shipping. The damage usually does not inhibit the product's usefulness; it is typically cosmetic.

11. **Odd-hours discount.** You may be able to get a discount if you agree to let vendors deliver during the sacred hours we talked about earlier—11:30 a.m. to 1:30 p.m. There may also be an opportunity to get a discount if you give your vendors access to your facility and let them **night drop** orders when no one is at your restaurant. If you're flexible, you may be able to pick up a nice piece of change over the long run.

12. **Proprietary-brand discount.** Some vendors will give you a price reduction if you purchase a large amount of their **proprietary brands.** For instance, Sysco and other similar purveyors will give you a **brand incentive** if you purchase a lot of its products that carry the Sysco label.

■ ASK AND YOU MIGHT RECEIVE

A lot of folks like to negotiate for better deals. There is nothing wrong with that, but the reality is, you can't be an effective negotiator if you don't have anything worthwhile to give up to the other side. If you're part of a gigantic restaurant corporation, all the negotiating has been done for you. The best deals have been made. Your job is to take advantage of them and devote the extra time you have to other business activities.

The rest of us have to take a different approach. We have to bug our purveyors, in a nice way of course, to keep us up to date on any deals they have right now that we may want to consider, or that they might have in the future. You should get into the habit of asking, "Is your company offering any promotions?"

Sometimes you get something just because you asked for it. Keep in mind that a lot of vendors will not always tell you about these things. They will usually open up only if they feel you are going to dump them. Then they go to the next script in their playbook and begin dickering with you. Try it. If you are a customer of the local cable company, call up and say you want to dump it. Then sit back and listen to all the deals that suddenly materialize.

We have a friend who is a long-time customer of an alarm service. One day, just out of the blue, someone asked him if he paid his alarm bill in advance. He said, "No, why would I?" Well, it turned out that if he paid one year in advance, he got one month free service. This worked out to about a 10 percent discount. He called the company, and the accounts receivable lady told him sure, they had that promotion for as long as she could remember. Our friend wasn't too happy.

You have to make it sound as if you are always looking elsewhere for good deals. Keep the vendors guessing. If they start taking you for granted, we guarantee that the AP prices you pay will slowly inflate. And the support functions you get will typically dwindle little by little—not so much that you'd notice right away, but one day you'll wake up and find that you're in the same boat as our friend was with his alarm company.

Sometimes the best deals come about when the vendor has something to sell that you don't use. But maybe you can use it if you think about it long enough. For instance, if you've never used monk fish on your menu before, it may be time to start. You can do it. That's why you're a chef, not a bean counter.

To be good at this game, you will have to move from vendor to vendor. You can't get too comfortable. You always have to be out there looking for deals. The vendors will fight back by trying to distribute items that you can get nowhere else. But business is business, and to keep yours, they will miraculously find all sorts of little enticements that will help you enhance your bottom line. If you just go along, you'll get hammered. Stay vigilant. Stay prosperous.

HOW DO VENDORS FIGURE OUT WHAT AP PRICES TO CHARGE?

Vendors' pricing methods aren't much different than ours. It seems to us that there are at least four approaches.

1. *AP price as a function of the vendor's costs of doing business.* This is the starting point. A vendor will take its cost of the product and add a markup sufficient to cover all other expenses plus the desired profit. It is similar to the way a chef would attempt to price the menu items he or she wants to offer. Like the vendor, though, the chef may not be able to use the prices calculated this way because they may not be competitive.

2. *AP price as a function of competitive pressure.* Once the vendor (or restaurateur) calculates prices using the first approach, it typically has to adjust them in order to be consistent with the competition. This is where it gets a little tricky. If the vendor (or restaurateur) can differentiate a product just a little bit from the competition, it may have a competitive advantage and, therefore, be able to charge a little more. For instance, the vendor who offers daily delivery may be able to get a higher AP price for the same product offered by the vendor who delivers only once a week. And the restaurateur who, for example, offers free souvenir glasses with certain beverages may be able to get a premium price.

This approach may work for some items, but not for others. Just like a menu, the vendor's product line contains items that have various profit potentials. And just like us, it has to carry all sorts of things because buyers may nix an order if it doesn't offer a wide variety of merchandise. That's why vendors push the high-profit items and downplay the cheaper ones, like we do when we push the moneymakers on our menu while simultaneously burying the low-margin ones in fine print.

3. *AP price as a function of supply and demand.* Supply and demand usually have the greatest impact on perishable food prices and on the prices of basic staples, such as bulk sugar, flour, and so forth. The vendor who sells primarily these types of things is subject to supply and demand pressure, having less opportunity to differentiate its business. It's similar to the average wheat farmer. Not much he or she can do to affect the price. It's also similar to the way we tend to price things like banquet room rentals, where we may bump up the price quite a bit during the wedding season when demand is super high, but give all kinds of concessions during the slow periods.

4. *AP price as a function of buyer pricing.* Without a doubt, vendors prefer this type of pricing procedure. Unfortunately, if you fall into this trap, you're almost certain to overpay. **Buyer pricing** comes about in one of two ways. One, it will happen when you don't have specifications; in this situation, the sales rep will "assist" you in developing them, which, of course, can be hazardous to your pocketbook. It is similar to the catering customer who arrives without having given much thought to what he or she wants. And two, it will happen if the buyer engages in panic buying. A restaurant customer may engage in panic buying if, for example, he or she insists on having dinner at a swanky restaurant and is willing to tip out everybody and their brother in order to get a last-minute reservation.

Pricing seems to us to be one of the last managerial arts. It is not based entirely on math formulas and computer printouts; hunches and experience usually come into play as well. The trick is to try to differentiate yourself from the competition so that you can charge enough to sustain your business. What's funny, though, is that after all is said and done, the average restaurant earns a net profit of only about 5 percent of its sales revenue (National Restaurant Association estimate) and the average vendor only about 1 percent to 3 percent of its sales revenue (Patt Patterson, "Finding 'Bargains'— and Knowing How to Police Them," *Nation's Restaurant News,* April 5, 1993, p. 37). In many cases, a vendor earns only a few pennies per unit sold (Michael L. Facciola, "Supply & Dementia," *Food Arts,* May 1992, p. 112). We suppose the moral of this story is: It's no good to be average; you have to be a whole heck of a lot better.

APPLY WHAT YOU'VE LEARNED

1. List two different uses for each of the following ingredients:

> Heavy whipping cream
> Flounder filets
> Mozzarella cheese
> Flank steak
> Valencia oranges
> Fresh strawberries
> Green cabbage
> Canned corn

2. How might the intended use of the following products affect the purchase order?

  a. Turkey
  b. Crabmeat
  c. Paper towels

DISCUSSION QUESTIONS

1. Describe the concept of *value* as it relates to purchasing.

2. Name a situation where the lowest AP price doesn't result in the lowest EP cost.

3. What should F & B buyers who want to maintain or improve quality focus on, and why? Give an example of how a sole focus on high quality can affect customer satisfaction.

4. What is the first step in going after the best possible deal?

5. When costing out recipes, how many versions should you have?

6. What are AP and EP? Which do you think is more important to monitor?

7. What are some ways that F & B buyers try to reduce the AP prices of products they purchase?

8. Name five types of discounts that buyers can receive from vendors, and describe them briefly.

6

ORDERING
PROCESS

How Do I Actually Buy This Stuff?

CHAPTER OUTLINE

- CATEGORIZE YOUR PRODUCTS
- ORDER SIZES
- ORDER RECORD
- CONTACT VENDORS
- TECHNOLOGY'S IMPACT ON PURCHASING

LEARNING OBJECTIVES

☑ Categorize products before ordering.

☑ Determine the optimal ordering size for products.

☑ Choose an ordering approach aligned with the organization's needs.

☑ Negotiate an ordering system with chosen purveyors.

☑ Close the deal.

☑ Prepare purchase records.

N ow that you know where the best deals are and how to get them, you have to gear up to order what you need. Most of the hard work is done. However, there are a few more decisions to make before we can close the book on the purchasing function.

CATEGORIZE YOUR PRODUCTS

Before determining the ordering procedures that will work best you should sort your products into three categories:

1. *Perishable products.* Anything that has a very short shelf life is considered perishable.

2. *Center-plate items; your most expensive ingredients.* Some of them, like frozen fish and some beverage alcohols, may have a fairly long shelf life, but most of them don't.

3. *Everything else.* This includes everything from paper products to canned tomatoes to the toothpicks that hold the garnish on the sandwiches.

You want to order the first two categories as frequently as possible. Daily delivery and daily ordering may be a bit much for everything, but given the nature of perishable products, you do not want them sitting around losing culinary quality. Freshness is very important. Center-plate items, especially the protein-based ones, are very expensive, so you also do not want them sitting around increasing your carrying costs. Some products, such as fresh meats, are usually perishable and expensive. These are the ones you especially want to pay close attention to.

The third category should be ordered as infrequently as your storage room and pocketbook allow. These are typically your less expensive items that have long shelf lives. In some cases, such as paper napkins, the shelf life is almost limitless. By ordering them infrequently, you can spend more time looking for deals and tracking the expensive ingredients. You don't want to be bogged down ordering canned goods, paper products, and sugar packets every week. You have enough to do. And these items are usually not so expensive that they drive up your carrying costs.

ORDER SIZES

For the first two categories, the best approach is to adopt a *use-based* system of ordering. This process includes the following steps:

1. Take a physical inventory (physical count) of the items you have on hand. This is typically done first thing Monday morning. More frequently if necessary. *Warning:* don't order anything unless you know how much of it you already have. It's OK to have four bottles of lemon pepper in your home kitchen cabinet, but not OK in your restaurant. Second warning: Always make sure that the quality of what you have on hand has not deteriorated to the point where it cannot be served. A lot of things do not necessarily spoil,

but you wouldn't want to serve them. It's OK to serve rusty lettuce at home, but not OK in your restaurant.

2. Forecast your needs for the upcoming period. This period should be no longer than one week. For some items, such as bread and dairy, it may be one day.

3. Calculate the amount of product you expect to use during the upcoming period.

4. Subtract what you have on hand.

5. Finally, add a little safety stock so that you don't run out.

Let's look at a typical example: precut sirloin steaks. If you anticipate serving 600 of them next week, and you have 25 on hand, you would order 575 plus a few more just to be on the safe side. *Note:* Oftentimes, you will find that you will automatically add a **safety stock** when calculating order sizes because you can't always order the exact amount of what you want. For instance, if the sirloin steaks you use are packed 12 to 14 per case, or an average of 13 per case, you can't order $44\frac{1}{4}$ cases ($575 \div 13$ = approx. $44\frac{1}{4}$ cases). You'll have to order 45 cases. It's like having a built-in safety stock feature (or built-in extra waste feature, depending on your point of view).

For the third category, the best approach is to adopt a *par-stock* system of ordering. This process includes the following steps:

1. Determine how much of the product you are most likely to use during the next three to six months. This amount will be the **par stock.** Three months is a good number for things like canned goods and most frozen products. However, you don't want to hang on to these products too long, especially the frozen ones, because freezing does not stop quality deterioration, it merely slows it down. Six months is good for things like sugar packets, paper products, and salt.

2. Set a minimum amount of product you should always have on hand. When you reach this amount of inventory you will need to order it. This minimum is roughly equal to the amount of product you think you will use during the lead-time.

3. Subtract the minimum—the amount you have on hand— from the par stock to come up with the order size.

PURCHASING'S LINK TO MAINTENANCE

In almost every case, purchasing is responsible for securing outside service contractors for the entire restaurant operation.

Let's look at a typical example: cocktail napkins. Here's an item you don't want to order every time you turn around. A three- to six-month supply won't spoil. Staff won't steal it (though there's a tendency to waste the product when people see so much of it lying around). And you'll save money because the quantity discounts for stuff like paper products are usually very generous—much greater than the carrying charges you'll incur for holding a large amount of it in inventory.

ORDER RECORD

You should always have a record of what you order. You will need it when the shipment arrives. If you don't know what you ordered you will have nothing to guide you when you inspect the shipment. Mistakes occur regularly. It's not uncommon to receive the wrong brand of a product, nor is it unusual to find that the shipment contains the wrong product size. Heck, it might not even be your order in the first place; at the college at least once a semester one of the liquor vendors tries to deliver the Performing Arts Center's liquor order to us. Furthermore, if you have an order record you will know when something hasn't come in and can get on the horn to find out what's happening.

CONTACT VENDORS

Once you have your order sketched out, you need to contact the appropriate purveyor. There are several ways to do this:

1. *Use e-mail or the Web.* This is especially useful if you are buying direct from the manufacturer. It is also a good method if you are part of a large restaurant corporation

and you order things from the company's commissary or central distribution center. These days it is also becoming more common to use this method to contact local vendors. The nice thing about the Internet is that you can get all the information you need in one place. It is always open for business. You know immediately what the purveyors have on hand and if something is on back order. And you can transact your business quickly and easily.

2. *Telephone.* A lot of chefs like to use the phone. They want the human contact, someone they can reach in an emergency situation, someone they can complain to if necessary. Many do not trust what they see on the Internet, especially if they've been disappointed in the past. Plus, if you don't have an expensive computer and high-speed access, the Internet can be slow going. *Warning:* The phone is time-consuming, particularly if you like to gossip with the order desk. Also, mistakes are more likely when you use this ordering method.

3. *Fax machine.* This bit of technology revolutionized the ordering process. It permits buyers to check off on a piece of paper those items they want and then submit this information instantaneously over the phone lines. This was the first time that you were almost assured that there would be no misunderstandings. Furthermore, since the machine's printed output can be stored for historical records, it can be used to verify orders, prove they were sent, and establish usage patterns that can help you do a better job of forecasting your needs in the future. Of course, the computer offers these advantages, and more; however, the computer is a more expensive option.

4. *In person.* It is rare for sales reps to come around regularly to the typical restaurant to write up orders. It may happen the first time or two you do business with that vendor, but it is not a common occurrence. Sales reps normally come around to schmooze, or to introduce new products. At that time they will be glad to write an order if you have one. **Brokers,** people who work on a sales commission basis for vendors who do not have their own sales forces, tend to come around much more frequently than sales reps.

5. *Will-call buying.* If you are a small stop, you may have to rely on this method for some things. There are two ways to do it. You can send in your order, say by sending a fax or

leaving a message on voice mail, and then stop on the way to work to pick it up. Or you can just show up and go shopping, which is typical if you do a lot of business with places like Sam's Club or Costco. The first method is a little more convenient because the completed order is waiting for you. You just pay and go. This is the way it usually works if you go to the vendor's warehouse to pick up something.

6. *Standing order.* You make your order when the driver shows up. After a while, the driver knows approximately how much product you'll need to last until he or she comes around again. It's very convenient. But this method is not available for most things you buy. You may still be able to bargain for it for things like dairy, bread, breakfast pastries, soda pop syrup, and other similar items.

7. *Farmers' market.* Depending on where you are, this option may be available. Alternately, in some cities there is a *water market* area where foods come in from around the world about 3:00 or 4:00 in the morning and buyers from the large hotels, clubs, restaurants, and supermarkets can tag what they want delivered to their properties. Or they can tag things, pay for them, load them in their vans, and go. Although anyone can visit a *farmers' market,* this may not be the case with these water markets. One potential advantage of these markets is that you can save a bit of money by avoiding an intermediary and providing several of your own support functions, such as your own delivery. Another advantage is that you may get first crack at the best, freshest products.

8. *Auctions.* If you're in the market for small wares, equipment, and so forth, they say that if you know what you are doing you can find some super good deals at a live auction site or an online site such as eBay. You can also find some items through a process called a **reverse auction.** This is where you go on the Internet and let it be known that you want to buy "X." Vendors then start "bidding" for your business. For instance, one might offer to sell it to you for $100. Another vendor might pop in and bid $99. And so on. At the end of the auction deadline you take the one with the lowest bid. If you get involved in auctions, though, you have to spend a lot of time. And, with the reverse auction, your specifications better be textbook perfect.

TECHNOLOGY'S IMPACT ON PURCHASING

Technology has come a long way in the past 25 years. Here are some of the key developments that have made ordering, inventory control, and the rest of the purchasing process much easier.

▣ FAX MACHINE

One of the first technological revolutions in purchasing was the introduction of a cost-effective fax (facsimile) machine in the 1980s. This single piece of office equipment revolutionized the order-taking and -receiving process. It permitted buyers to check off on a piece of paper those items they wanted to purchase and then to submit this information instantaneously over the telephone lines. This process significantly reduced the confusion and mistakes sometimes associated with verbal orders. Furthermore, since a fax machine's printed output could be stored for historical records, it was used to verify orders, prove they were sent, and establish usage patterns. However, as many folks soon realized, the thermal paper that fax machines originally used had a limited lifespan. This problem was solved in the 1990s with the introduction of fax machines that used plain paper and could store numerous faxes for distribution at off-peak hours. Today, fax machines can use the Internet to send and receive documents, thereby significantly reducing the costs associated with long distance calls.

▣ PERSONAL COMPUTER (PC)

Although fax machines are still a very common tool that restaurant operations use to order products and services, PCs are quickly overtaking the duties of this office workhorse. Today, many restaurant operators embrace the digital world.

The PC is by far the most powerful and useful technological tool a chef can have, even if it is a stand-alone machine not connected to other computers or to the Internet. For instance, previously the majority of inventory costing and counting was done by hand by individuals armed with calculators, paper, and pencils. PCs have made this process much less time-consuming and more stress-free. PCs have also made it possible for chefs to base their purchasing decisions on current data, thus minimizing the need to estimate such items as current food costs and menu item popularity.

▦ POINT-OF-SALE (POS) SYSTEM

Before the introduction of the computerized POS system, it was very difficult to track sold menu items. The gear-driven cash register merely stores cash and provides some limited sales information on printed receipts. Today, POS systems use PCs and are highly integrated in the daily functions of operations. These systems can tabulate and organize tremendous amounts of sales data very quickly.

Most POS systems now feature touch-screen technology. They also permit users to delete menu items, track employee activity, analyze worker productivity, and force **order modifiers** (e.g., when a food server enters a steak order, the computer asks, "What temperature?" or when the food server enters a baked potato order, the computer asks, "Butter and sour cream with that?"). Some advanced POS systems even allow a server to carry a wireless ordering system to the table; orders entered this way are automatically sent to the display screen in the bar and/or kitchen.

In most restaurant operations, POS systems are networked and communicate with a central computer, referred to as a **server.** This server can track sales from the connected computers in all departments or areas within the restaurant and instantly provide vital information to managers. Advanced POS systems integrate with inventory-tracking systems that automatically delete from inventory the standard amount of each ingredient that is used to make each menu item. The integration of POS and inventory systems provides the chef with a theoretical inventory usage figure that can later be compared with actual physical counts. Furthermore, some POS systems facilitate the ability to permit purchase orders to be drafted directly to the distributors, based on sales and inventory reduction information.

▦ BAR CODES

Some restaurant operations place **bar codes** on their inventory items (or use those the distributors applied) to streamline the inventory-control process. Bar code labels are vertical lines of varying thicknesses separated by blank space. These lines and spaces, or *elements,* are used to provide a bar code reader with an **identification code (ID).** This ID is then used to look up the product on a database. **Bar code elements,** IDs, and corresponding product information are based on a standard that associates these pieces of information. The most commonly used standard is the Universal Product Code (UPC). However, other standards, such as EAN, Codabar, and Code 128, are also in use.

▩ ONLINE ORDERING

Several software companies specializing in the use of the Internet have developed **online ordering systems** that permit buyers to order products over the Internet. These e-procurement applications streamline and minimize a buyer's ordering procedure, thereby creating a value-added service for the buyer. At the same time, when a buyer uses this ordering system, he or she helps streamline the order-taking process at the distributor's end. Previously, a distributor had to enter a buyer's order from a fax, telephone call, or written purchase order, but with the new system, the inefficiencies of the multiple-ordering process are eliminated. Instead, a buyer enters the order on an e-marketplace and sends it directly to the distributor. This process reduces labor costs and time on both the buyer's and the distributor's end. Another distributor benefit of the process is the likelihood that users of this ordering system will get so comfortable with a distributor's system that they will stop shopping around and become **house** (i.e., **prime-vendor) accounts.**

These **e-marketplaces** also allow buyers and distributors to negotiate contractual pricing agreements on selected products prior to ordering. Buyers and distributors who join an e-marketplace have an instant line of communication to negotiate products and prices. Buyers begin this process by searching for an item they are interested in purchasing and identifying vendors who offer this product. The buyers then submit a request for quote (RFQ) from these vendors. Distributors then make an offer, and the buyer chooses the desired vendor.

After pricing arrangements have been set, buyers can allow department managers or other staff to order items directly from the vendor through the e-marketplace. This method of ordering minimizes the time between when an order is placed and authorized. Authorized individuals are given an account and can order specific products as long as these orders do not exceed a designated spending limit. For example, a sous chef might be able to order certain foods on the e-marketplace without writing out a purchase requisition or purchase order as long as the total amount purchased at one time does not exceed $1,000.

Product information on e-marketplaces can typically be retrieved in several ways, unlike the typical printed catalog in which everything is listed alphabetically and/or by product categories. For instance, databases on the e-marketplace enable buyers to search for and evaluate all of the types of hot dogs a particular vendor sells.

Buyers might view hot dogs by size, types of ingredients, and pack-ers' brands. They can also narrow the search, for example, to 4:1 (four hot dogs per pound), pure-beef, Oscar Mayer brand hot dogs. From this list, they can then choose the desired product or continue to refine and narrow the search. Once buyers find the desired prod-uct, they can then choose (i.e., *tag*) products they want to procure or submit for a RFQ.

If an order is acceptable to the buyer, it can be transmitted right on the computer. The buyer can also attach a note telling the ven-dor more specific information. The order is then instantly commu-nicated to the vendor, who might send this information to a local distribution center for processing and delivery.

■ INVENTORY CONTROL SOFTWARE APPLICATIONS

Today, many restaurant operators use some type of computer ap-plication to increase their inventory and cost control efforts. For ex-ample, some operators develop elaborate spreadsheets using generic spreadsheet software, such as Microsoft Excel®, through which they list all of their products in inventory and then develop mathemati-cal formulas to calculate costs and usage.

On the last day of each month, chefs physically count their store-room and in-process inventories and enter this information on the spreadsheet. They also enter all AP prices, which usually come from typing in invoice receipts for the month or from directly down-loading them from an online ordering system they are using. The computer then uses this information to calculate the value of the month's ending inventory.

The computer already has the month's beginning inventory stored in memory, since last month's ending inventory is this month's be-ginning inventory.

Once the major variables have been entered (beginning inven-tory, ending inventory, purchases, and other end-of-month adjust-ments), the computer can easily calculate the actual cost of goods sold for that month.

Some restaurant operators use off-the-shelf software packages and services that are specifically designed to manage inventory in a restaurant environment. These software packages can streamline the back-of-the-house operation. Many of them can be linked to an operator's POS system.

Some of these packages can also cost recipes, analyze a recipe's nutritional information, calculate standard (i.e., "expected") food and beverage costs, evaluate a food item's sales history, forecast sales, develop audit trails, allow instant stock-level information, and enhance menu planning efforts. In addition, many of these software packages can track employee work schedules, attendance patterns, and work-hour accumulations.

When generic spreadsheet programs or off-the-shelf software do not meet a chef's needs, the restaurant might hire a software consulting firm that specializes in the hospitality industry. A specialist can develop customized software applications to satisfy almost any need. Alternately, the developers of some off-the-shelf software products can customize some or all of their standard software packages.

■ WHAT LIES AHEAD?

It is hard to believe that the use of technology in the restaurant industry, especially for the inventory control and purchasing functions, is only in its infancy. In the future, technology will bring more ideas, tools, and information to restaurant operators. And it cannot come too soon—since restaurants will continue to experience more competitive markets, slimmer profit margins, and a shrinking labor force. Technology will help chefs to overcome these obstacles and will, ultimately, contribute to the success of their businesses.

In a competitive environment, chefs have less time to make key managerial decisions. Making the correct decision quickly can be done, but only if managers have access to the necessary technological tools.

In the future, **distributors** will probably bear more of the burden of providing restaurant operators with the proper technology to suit a more technical, mechanical purchasing process, as well as the burden of helping operators control their businesses more efficiently. Since restaurant businesses are the distributors' customers, it is in their best interest to ensure that these companies make the correct purchasing and other key management decisions. Distributors, therefore, will be more actively involved with their customers, helping them to develop and evaluate new menus, substitution possibilities, inventory management procedures, and marketing strategies. They will also help restaurants continue streamlining the business process through the use of electronic commerce.

In the future, the distinguishing factors between distributors most likely will not be so much the products they sell—the major products are already very close in quality and cost—but the support functions they provide and the technology they use and can share with restaurant operators. In addition, because of time constraints, competition, and economies of scale, many industry experts think that more restaurant operators will practice one-stop shopping, thereby teaming with prime vendors to enhance each other's competitive positions.

WE'RE NOT DONE YET

Well, the order is in. The shipment is due to arrive soon. It's time for us to complete the cycle and discuss how to control these products between the time they show up at your back door until the time we sell them to happy guests. Let's turn to the final chapter and find out how to do that.

APPLY WHAT YOU'VE LEARNED

1. You are the executive chef/co-owner of a casual, limited-menu pub in downtown Miami. Due to a recent positive restaurant review, your business has been significantly higher than usual—sales revenue and cover counts during the past three weeks have doubled, and you have no doubt that this trend will continue. You are thinking about increasing the par stocks of most of your food items, especially the basic staples. Based on the following bar menu and the list of basic food ingredients noted below, adjust the par stocks to the level you feel is necessary to accommodate the increase in business while simultaneously avoiding stockouts. Explain your reasoning.

Bar Menu

Rosemary Grilled Chicken with Garlic Smashed Red Potatoes
and Steamed Sugar Snap Peas

12-ounce Strip Steak with Baked Potato, Steak Fries,
or Steamed Sugar Snap Peas

8-ounce Black Angus Burger on a Toasted Kaiser
with Lettuce, Tomato, Onion, and Dill Pickle
(Substitute a Garden Burger at no Extra Cost!)

Grilled Chicken Sandwich on a Toasted Kaiser
with Lettuce, Tomato, Onion, and Dill Spear
(Add your choice of Provolone, Cheddar,
American, or Swiss to any sandwich)

Dinner-Sized Deluxe Salad of Baby Field Greens, Tomato,
Onion, and Croutons, with your choice of unlimited addition:
shredded cheese, crumbled bacon, hard-boiled egg
(Add a half-pound grilled chicken, shrimp, or steak to your salad)

Current Par Stocks

Boneless, skinless chicken breasts, 6 ounce	11 cases
Garlic powder	3 jars
Red potatoes	3 50-pound bags
Sugar snap peas	3 15-pound bags
Cryovac 12-ounce strip steaks	8 cases
Russet potatoes	5 25-pound bags
Sweet potatoes	2 25-pound bags
Black Angus ground beef	50 pounds
Kaiser rolls	20 dozen
Garden burgers, 6 ounce	1 case
Cheese, Provolone, sliced	3 pounds
Cheese, Cheddar, sliced	2 pounds
Cheese, American, sliced	¾ pounds
Cheese, Swiss, sliced	1 pound
Lettuce, iceberg	6 heads
Lettuce, romaine	15 heads
Tomato, beefsteak	6 flats
Onion, red	1 25-pound bag

Dill pickle spears	1 bucket
Croutons	10-pound box
Eggs, grade A large in shell	12 dozen
Bacon, thin sliced	8 pounds
Shrimp, raw, frozen, 100 count, peeled, deveined, tail off	5 pounds

2. Assume that your storage facilities cannot accommodate the increased par stocks you calculated in question 1. What can you do to ensure that you don't have stockouts of these food products?

DISCUSSION QUESTIONS

1. What should an F & B buyer do before determining the ordering procedures that will work best for an operation?

2. What is the best way to order products that are not perishable or center-plate? Describe the steps in this ordering process.

3. How can a chef determine the par stock time period for non-perishable, non–center-plate items?

4. What are some ways to contact a purveyor after the order is sketched out?

5. With the recent rise of eBay and similar Web sites, auctions have become big business in the global economy. How do auctions work for F & B buyers? What products are they most suited to? Explain how it works.

INVENTORY
CONTROL

How Do I Keep Track of All This Stuff?

CHAPTER OUTLINE

- PURCHASE REQUISITION
- STOCK REQUISITION
- SPECIFICATIONS
- STANDARD RECIPES
- MAXIMUM INVENTORY TO KEEP ON HAND
- VENDOR APPROVAL
- ORDER RECORD
- KICKBACKS
- STEWARD SALES
- RECEIVING PROCEDURES
- STORAGE
- PHYSICAL INVENTORY
- DIRECT CONTROL SYSTEM

LEARNING OBJECTIVES

☑ Set up an inventory control system.

☑ Know how product specifications and standardized recipes contribute to inventory control systems.

☑ Determine how much inventory an operation should keep on hand.

☑ Explain the ethical and legal consequences of kickbacks and detect their presence.

☑ Manage steward sales.

☑ Navigate the vendor approval process.

☑ Conduct a physical inventory.

☑ Use inventory control to keep theft, waste, and pilferage at acceptable levels.

The best deals in the world won't amount to much if you do not have a system in place to ensure that the products you purchase are controlled between the time you check them in at the back door to the time you sell them and collect the sales revenue. The purchasing cycle is not complete until you turn those items back into cash. And to do that you need to pay very close attention to all the little things that can have a negative impact on your bottom line.

Let's take a peek at some of the things that you should consider when setting up an effective inventory control system.

PURCHASE REQUISITION

A **purchase requisition** is not something you usually find in use in a typical restaurant. It is more commonly seen in the large hotel food and beverage operations where extensive control procedures are in place.

The purchase requisition is similar to the **purchase order.** Actually, it precedes the purchase order. It is usually used to ask the buyer to purchase something that is not normally part of the regular inventory.

For instance, if you continually purchase frozen chicken breasts, there is no need for someone to fill out a purchase requisition. But if you don't regularly purchase this product, the purchase requisition is a good idea. It forces someone to do a little homework. He or she has to clarify the need for the item and include specification information. In other words, someone has to think about the purchase a little bit instead of just popping into the chef's office on the spur of the moment and asking for a special order.

The purchase requisition is also a good way to track things that are outside your normal inventory control system. Many times the items listed on the purchase requisition are going to be used for daily specials or private parties. A separate record of the products will help ensure that you calculate all the relevant costs for these events.

STOCK REQUISITION

In large properties that have a controlled access storage facility managed by a separate department head, the **stock requisition** is a common document used to track inventory. It is similar to the purchase requisition, in that someone fills out what is needed, but instead of giving the requisition to the buyer it is given to the storeroom manager, who then issues the products. For instance, if you are a room chef in a large hotel you would have to prepare these requisitions regularly, probably every day.

A big advantage of purchase requisitions and stock requisitions is the cost information they can generate. For instance, if someone has the time to cost them out each day, it can provide invaluable up-to-date food and beverage cost information. If you work on a tight food cost percentage, these data are essential. You need to know immediately, for example, if your food costs are on track so that you can make any necessary changes right now. If you have to wait for the official end-of-month accounting statement, the information is too old to help you. You may have blown your budget without even realizing it.

SPECIFICATIONS

Although specifications are used primarily to control product quality, they can also help you control product cost. If everyone is following the same specifications, the cost and quality should be consistent. This makes it easier for you to predict what will happen. The more predictability, the easier it will be to forecast the future.

STANDARD RECIPES

These serve the same quality and cost control purposes as specifications. And like specifications, *standard recipes* are absolutely necessary.

We're usually pretty good at maintaining a standard recipe file, since the culinary instructors kept beating it into our heads. Or if we are part of a large restaurant company, these files are typically kept up to date by the corporate chef and can be accessed electronically. Where we get lazy is when, out of the blue, we want to add a special on tonight's menu because we got such a good deal on a product we usually don't use in the restaurant. But before you add this menu item, take a few moments to sketch out a standard recipe for it. Also, take the time to cost it out, at least cost out the primary (most expensive) ingredients. Leave it on the side of your desk, or save it to your computer desktop, temporarily. If the special looks promising, you can go back later and formalize the recipe and add it to the file. If it doesn't generate positive vibes, you can delete it. The point is: Don't pick up the knife until you have a plan. If people love the special and you don't have anything written down, you're dead. You can't depend on your memory to help recreate what you did. In our crazy life we're lucky if we remember where we parked our cars.

MAXIMUM INVENTORY TO KEEP ON HAND

There are several rules of thumb in our business that you can follow to determine how much inventory you should keep on hand. Here are the three most common guidelines for **inventory control:**

1. The value of your food inventory should not exceed one week's food cost.

2. Your total inventory (food, beverage alcohol, and nonfood supplies) should not exceed 1 percent of your annual sales revenue.

3. The food inventory should not exceed one-third of the monthly food cost.

Let's assume your total annual sales revenue is $2,000,000, of which $500,000 is beverage alcohol sales revenue and $1,500,000 is food sales revenue. Let's also assume that your food cost is 24 percent, or $360,000 ($1,500,000 × .24) per year.

If you like rule 1, the food inventory on hand should not exceed $6,923. That is because the average weekly food cost is $6,923 ($360,000 ÷ 52 weeks).

With rule 2, the total inventory of all goods in your property should not exceed $20,000 ($2,000,000 × .01).

Rule number 3 suggests that your food inventory should be no more than $10,000 ($360,000 ÷ 12 months × 1/3).

Most chefs prefer rule number 1. If you follow this rule of thumb, it will be easier to meet your food cost percentage goal. When you run a tight inventory, the food turns faster, there is less spoilage and, therefore, less waste. Also, when you run lean and mean, there isn't a lot of stuff sitting around that could tempt someone with sticky fingers. Furthermore, if there isn't a lot of stuff all over the place, everyone is a little more careful with what they have. They trim things a little closer, they don't waste as much, they don't use the bar towel for only one wipe and toss it into the hamper. You get the idea.

One problem with maintaining this rigid guideline is the reluctance to lock up good deals that would require you to buy huge amounts of merchandise. Another potential difficulty is the likelihood that you will run out of some things; the number of stockouts may increase. Furthermore, if one of your staff worries about running out, he or she might unconsciously reduce the standard portion sizes a little in order to hoard enough product to serve everyone.

We certainly want to run a tight ship. And we realize that for the small operator, the name of the game is running a positive cash flow. But personally, we cannot accept stockouts. In our opinion, they are one of the worst things that can happen in a restaurant. You can't tell guests that you're sorry, you don't have their steak dinners tonight, but if they swing by tomorrow morning you'll have them ready for pickup. There is no such thing as a back order in our business; we're not running bookstores. We realize that this will cost a little more in the long run. That is why we account for it when we cost out recipes. We think a slightly higher menu price is much, much better than a stockout. That is why we tend to favor rule number 3 when dealing strictly with food.

We also cannot pass up good deals. Most of us in this business operate small restaurants and catering operations. For us, a few pennies here and there will add up to a huge number over the long term. Also, for folks like us, there are very few cost-cutting opportunities. Other than firing someone to cut costs (and, unfortunately, cutting service quality), sniffing out and grabbing good deals is the best, most productive way to save money.

Rule number 2 comes into play if you are responsible for the beverage inventory and the direct operating supplies inventory (things such as dish machine chemicals, paper products, linen, and so forth). Usually the restaurant manager or a separate bar manager is responsible for the beverage inventory. And in larger places, there is an executive steward overseeing most or all of the nonfood supplies. But if you have to control everything, rule number 2 works pretty well. Like rule number 3, it gives you a little leeway.

Let's review this carefully before we move on. Rule 1 will tend to save money in the long run and enhance your cash flow. If you are in a very competitive restaurant market, you may have to adopt this strategy. The other rules will cost you a bit more in the long run. But they are safer; they are more customer-friendly.

Sometimes we can overanalyze these situations. Many large restaurant companies have a gazillion formulas to track inventory and food costs. They have it down to a science. If you're a few cents off on food cost, someone will be calling you the next day wanting to know why you're off target and what you plan to do about it. But although it's great to save as much as possible, keep in mind that the way to make the big money in the restaurant business is not necessarily to cut every cost to the bone, but to fill the room with happy customers, with lots of them waiting in line to get in. If you can jump start the sales revenue figure, then a few extra expense dollars won't have much impact. Like they say, a full house cures many ills.

VENDOR APPROVAL

▪ APPROVED SUPPLIER LIST

It's unlikely that you will be the only one purchasing everything you need for the restaurant. You might start out that way, but sooner or later you will get other staff members involved with the ordering process. For instance, you may decide that the restaurant manager should take care of front-of-the house purchases. But before you delegate this responsibility, make sure you are the only one who determines which vendors to order from. If someone else will do part of the buying, you want to put them in a position where all they have to do is order. You don't mind if they shop around, but you don't want them straying from the approved supplier list unless you authorize it.

If you are part of a large, multiunit restaurant company, you typically will have a list like this to work from. If you want to add another purveyor to the list, you would have to get corporate approval before doing so.

▪ VENDOR APPROVAL PROCESS

Before other purveyors can be added to the approved supplier list, there should be a process used to check them out. Go to Chapter 3 of this book and use the criteria noted there to perform this examination. This is very important. Don't get in the habit of adding vendors impulsively. It's OK to add a vendor temporarily, to do it for one purchase, as this may be a good way to check out a potential purveyor's capability. But you don't want to risk adding a deceptive vendor who may collude with some of your staff members to rip you off. Or worse, adding a phantom vendor who will send you bills for nonexistent shipments and/or services.

■ APPROVED-PAYEE LIST

An **approved-payee list** is a list of all persons and companies eligible to receive a payment from your restaurant. It is similar to the **approved-supplier list** (which pertains only to vendors). The two usually go hand-in-hand, whereby an approved supplier is automatically added to the disbursements (approved-payee) list.

Most chefs don't get involved in the bill-paying process. However, many of them influence who gets on the list since they are the ones who regularly check out new vendors. Because of this, both lists are continually revised, usually because of a decision the chef made.

The vendors most likely to be added and subtracted from these lists are food vendors. There are a few nonfood supplies vendors to choose from, but not nearly as many of them as there are for food. For beverage alcohol, the vendors never change, or change very infrequently. Chances are, if there's any controversy with a vendor, it will be a food vendor, and any blame will be placed at the chef's doorstep. Be careful.

ORDER RECORD

As mentioned earlier in this text, you absolutely, positively, beyond a shadow of a doubt, have to know what you ordered so that you can use this information to inspect shipments. You don't necessarily have to have copies of formal purchase orders. You can scribble on legal size yellow sheets if you want to. Just do it.

A lot of vendors try to make this task easy for you by letting you go on their Web sites to enter your orders. You can save copies of these orders on your desktop for future use, or you can print out hard copies and leave them in the receiving area. If you use these formats, though, don't get too comfortable. Since the vendors are likely to take your information and run all sorts of useful statistics for you, it may lull you into the comfort zone. This is especially true if they will cost out your standard recipes for you (using their products, of course). Forget that. Don't get lazy.

KICKBACKS

A **kickback** is an illegal rebate. It's an illegal gift given by a vendor to someone if he or she will agree to help defraud the restaurant. It can be very easy to pull this off. Repeat: very easy.

One way to avoid any compromising situation is to do all of the buying yourself. But that isn't always practical. Others eventually will get involved.

Fortunately, the educated, experienced chef of today is much harder to fool than the restaurant owner who is a retired doctor, who thought getting into the business would be a lot of fun (fun for everyone but the doctor). The good chefs know what to look for. It's much harder to trick them.

Let's consider the most typical kickback, the one where a buyer agrees to pay a certain AP price for a product of a certain quality, but agrees to accept a quality that is just a bit lower. The price paid, then, is slightly higher than it should be. It's a very subtle fraud. It's not obvious to the untrained eye. You can fool a lot of people who don't know their food inside and out, but these days, given the increased education and culinary training that exists in our industry, it's not easy to slip this one past the chef.

If you have someone in your operation doing some of the buying, you should check what the buyer is ordering and see if the AP prices are about right for that quality of product. Now sometimes a person will order and pay more for something because the vendor provides superior support functions. If that's the case, no problem. You can't micromanage in the restaurant business: it doesn't work very well. However, you have to stay out of the office and walk the racetrack. Your presence alone will go a long way to discourage illicit activity.

STEWARD SALES

Steward sales refers to sales of your inventory to employees. You charge them the price you paid. In effect, you allow them to take advantage of your purchasing power, such as it is, for their personal benefit.

Most of the big companies won't do this, so for them it's a non-issue. But if you're an independent operation, you might consider offering it as an employee perk. We should tell you, though, that this procedure can be very time consuming. It also can complicate your inventory control and accounts receivable functions. Furthermore, if you let employees drop in any time they want and pick up something, you could end up with stockouts before your next delivery date.

These sales may take a lot of time, effort, and thought. And don't forget risk. The staff may get the idea that you're not overly concerned about inventory control. For instance, if employees regularly leave the property with products, it can be viewed as routine. Eventually, no one will check to see if an employee taking something home has a property pass signed by the chef or another manager. This may increase pilferage.

We wouldn't stay away from steward sales altogether, but we would place some limits on them. For instance, you might let only the management staff take advantage of this perk. Or if you open it up to everyone, you might restrict what can be purchased by employees as well as the times of the year they can purchase. A well-known, upscale hotel chain allows employees to tack on a personal mattress to the hotel's periodic order of replacement mattresses. The purchase price is incredibly low and the quality is incredibly high. A great perk. And it really doesn't cost the hotel much, just a little time.

RECEIVING PROCEDURES

This is usually the time when we take ownership of the goods purchased. A mistake here can be very costly. It's your responsibility to ensure that you begin protecting the items. You don't want to go through all the trouble of finding great deals only to lose the advantage at this point.

It's easy to get sidetracked when a shipment arrives. It seems that many deliveries come at the wrong time. Typically, we're involved in one catastrophe or another and don't always have time to do this work adequately. But you have to force yourself to pay attention because it is easy to screw up. And if you don't do it right, the drivers will notice it; some of them will try to rip you off if they think you're not focused on the receiving function.

Some chefs delegate the receiving responsibility to a staff member. This is OK if the employee knows what to look for and is not there just to count and weigh products. If he or she is not familiar with product quality characteristics, if he or she can't recite long passages by heart from *The Professional Chef,* or similar text, you better train that person well or do all receiving yourself.

Think of the receiving function as similar to the expeditor position. The typical chef oftentimes prefers to handle this activity personally. Or, if it's delegated to someone, usually it's a person with a great deal of experience and familiarity with the restaurant's expectations. Sounds to us like a job requirement for the receiving agent.

Your receiving process should incorporate the following procedures:

1. *When the shipment arrives, compare the invoice to your order record.* You would be amazed at how many times things are delivered that you didn't order. Occasionally you will get the shipment that's slated for the restaurant down the road. The shipment, order record, and invoice must match.

2. *Check the product quality.* Everything you order must meet your specifications. It's easy for the vendor to mistakenly ship an off-spec product. It's also easy for the untrained eye to accept, say, canned diced tomatoes instead of canned diced tomatoes packed in tomato puree. Little things like that will screw up your production cycle. Sometimes you need to tear open a package to check quality. For instance, it wouldn't hurt to tear open a sample of Cryovac-packed lamb chops to determine if spoilage bacteria are present. When you check quality, make sure to note expiration dates. These are easy to miss if you don't know what to look for or where they are typically printed on the package.

3. *Check the quantity.* Count and weigh items, as necessary. Short counts are easy to overlook if you're in a hurry. You must always weigh the protein items purchased by the pound as well as spot-checking the portion-cut ones. Make sure you have a scale that's checked and calibrated regularly. Lots of folks don't bother to weigh things, nor do they count everything. If that's the case, pretty soon you'll

be getting 24 napkins in your bundles instead of 25. Don't take anything for granted. If the driver is out to screw you over, he or she will fiddle with the quality and the quantity. Don't get lazy. Do your job.

4. *Spot check AP prices on the invoice and compare them to the quoted ones listed on the order record.* Occasionally there is a discrepancy. Usually this happens when the vendor forgets to factor in a discount. If you have a bookkeeper on your staff you can forgo this part of the receiving process and let him or her check prices later on.

5. *Accept the shipment, assuming everything is OK.* You will need to sign a copy of the invoice and keep a copy.

6. *If you have to reject all or part of a shipment, you have to make sure that you get the proper credit.* The driver may be able to reprice the invoice right then and there. Or he or she might be able to give you a credit slip. However, if the shipment is delivered by a common carrier, you may have to phone the vendor, or e-mail or snail mail a credit memo to the vendor, in order to ensure that your account is credited.

7. *You may have to arrange to ship back all or part of the unacceptable shipment, but only if the driver works for a common carrier.* This is not unusual when you buy direct and bypass the intermediary. You can save money with direct buying, but when a problem with the shipment pops up, seemingly minor difficulties multiply rapidly.

8. *Move all acceptable shipments into storage as quickly as possible.* You don't want things sitting around too long, especially refrigerated and frozen merchandise. Also, you don't want things sitting around tempting people who have sticky fingers. Sometimes part or all of a shipment will bypass storage and go directly into production. For instance, a meat delivery may be slated for a private party that night and, therefore, go straight to the production kitchen.

9. *Complete whatever paperwork is needed.* Usually you can get by with merely sending your copy of the invoices and credit slips to the office where, before paying the monthly bill, the bookkeeper will reconcile them with the monthly statement that the vendor sends.

10. *If you are on a COD basis, send the driver to the office to pick up a check for the total price of the delivery.* Make sure the driver has the appropriate paperwork.

11. *If you maintain a computerized inventory file, someone will need to update the inventory amounts, any AP price changes, and bar codes.* (This assumes you make your own bar codes to tag incoming merchandise to make it easier to track it in storage.) Usually an office staff member handles these things.

12. *If the driver is required to pick up something from you, or is required to backhaul, say, recyclable materials you've been saving, the receiving agent usually helps load the truck.* He or she also sees to it that the driver gets all of the necessary paperwork and authorizations.

13. *If the drivers are route salespersons, the same receiving procedures should apply.* There's a tendency to get a little lazy when dealing with them. Don't let that happen to you. You shouldn't tempt these folks; they will take advantage of you if you beg them to rip you off.

14. The receiving process changes a bit if you have several shipments dropped off by the USPS, FedEx, DHL, or UPS. These carriers drop and go. For instance, they may leave a shipment at your back door and just ring the doorbell; by the time you open the door, they are gone. You still need to follow the procedures already noted, but you have to do everything yourself. There are no drivers to help you.

STORAGE

One of the major headaches most chefs live with is the lack of adequate storage. Insufficient space and inadequate equipment make it almost impossible to secure your products, minimize spoilage and other avoidable waste, and keep pilferage down to an acceptable level. It also can severely hamper your ability to make necessary menu changes and handle large groups of customers.

However, tight storage may be a good thing, since it forces you to work smarter. The chef who can produce hundreds of meals per day out of a small kitchen and storage facility, *and* keep tight control (especially of his or her sanity), has our respect.

Storage is an activity typically performed in conjunction with receiving. Often the same person who receives also stores. Ideally, you would like to separate these activities, but unless you operate a large property, such separation of duties is cost prohibitive. In the average restaurant, though, it's a nonissue, because you will be the one doing most everything associated with buying, receiving, and storing.

Your storage management process should incorporate the following procedures:

1. *Limited access is the primary defense against product loss due to theft or pilferage.* But in the typical restaurant it is impossible to limit access to everything you store. This is only possible in the big hotels and clubs that enjoy tremendous sales revenues, enough to support the large employee staff needed to make it work. For most of us, we have to adjust by limiting access to the storage areas in your operation that hold the expensive stuff that people love to steal—things like meats, fish, poultry, and beverage alcohol. You need to set up your production areas in such a way that you can lock up all your expensive ingredients and issue only enough to handle the shift's needs. All the other ingredients should be available in an open-storeroom area so that employees can help themselves. In essence, you track and control the steak, but let the peas take care of themselves. This method actually works pretty well. The expensive stuff usually represents about 80 percent of your total purchases. If you can control the big stuff, you have a pretty good handle on your costs. Furthermore, not too many people want to steal the peas.

2. *Make sure you have a good locking system.* In our opinion, the best physical locks are those manufactured by Medeco, and the best electronic locking system is the one manufactured by Marlok. We like Marlok especially, because it gives you the name of the most recent person who entered the locked facilities, as well as when he or she entered. Alarms are also a good idea. Not only will they deter thieves, but they can also be set up to warn you, for instance, that there is a problem with the freezer temperature. Don't forget to lock up after yourself. Don't get lazy and leave opened locks lying around where a dishonest employee can key

them or substitute a similar lock that he or she has a key for. And don't hand out the keys to everyone. There should be only three sets of keys: one for you, one for the restaurant manager, and a backup set in the safe.

3. *Use Web Cam security.* Strategically placed cameras are an effective security measure. They are also very efficient; their costs have shrunk dramatically to the point where they are easily affordable by even the smallest restaurant operation. You can have them set up to digitally record various parts of your operation. Plus, since they are accessible over the Internet, you can check on your operation from any location in the world that has Internet capability.

4. *Rotate stock.* **Stock rotation** is essential. Get in the habit of moving the older stock to the front of the shelf and placing the newer products behind them. You should practice the **FIFO** method, that is, *first-in, first-out,* in order to reduce spoilage and waste. If possible, purchase a **dot system,** such as Day Dots, or some similar product, to help you date and mark items in storage. In fact, depending on your local health district requirements, you may be required to date many items in storage to help prevent food-borne illness.

5. *Maintain proper temperature and humidity.* Shelf life can be enhanced or reduced, depending on the temperature and humidity levels in your storage areas. This is especially true for refrigerated and freezer storage. Have a maintenance person check these levels periodically; over the long run, the few dollars it costs to calibrate them will save you a great deal of spoilage and waste. You may be able to minimize this expense if you turn your inventory very rapidly. However, you don't want to risk getting a bad report from the health district sanitarian or disappointing a guest with food that's past its peak of quality.

6. *Ensure proper cleaning and sanitizing procedures are followed.* A clean environment will enhance shelf life. A dirty one will reduce it and draw the wrath of the health district sanitarian. You should think about having some of your staff members take the ServSafe course offered by the National Restaurant Association Educational Foundation (NRAEF), http://www.nraef.org/servsafe/, or some similar type of sanitation instruction. It can be taken online at their

convenience. This instruction is invaluable. If you attend a culinary school and have taken it as part of your curriculum requirements, you know how useful it is. It's thought that before too long, health districts throughout the country will require all food handlers to have a course like this instead of just going down to the health district and getting a health card after watching a couple of old movies about food-borne illness.

7. *Arrange inventory conveniently on the shelves.* You will need to take a physical inventory of everything in storage at least once a month. This is necessary so that an accurate actual-cost-of-food-sold figure can be calculated. To speed up the process, items should be laid out in such a way that the inventory-taking procedures can be done quickly and efficiently. A good pattern we like is to set up "grocery store" shelves, where all items face the front. This makes it easier to read the labels, and it also can deter pilferage since it gives the impression that someone is always paying attention to the inventory. There are different ways to do this, such as arranging things alphabetically, grouping them into different areas, and so forth. Whatever works best. Keep in mind that if things are tossed here and there, you will eventually neglect taking your month-end inventory. You will also have more waste and spoilage if products are not easily arranged to ensure that the FIFO system is being followed.

PHYSICAL INVENTORY

A **physical inventory** is an actual counting and valuing of products you have in your restaurant. It is very time-consuming, which means that you are going to be tempted to avoid doing it. Not too many of us feel like donning an overcoat and going into the walk-in freezers to count inventory.

But keeping track of what you have is the most essential aspect of inventory control. Follow our recommendations and you will stay on top of your product costs. There are three types of physical inventory procedures that we suggest.

■ MONTH-END PHYSICAL INVENTORY OF ALL FOOD ITEMS

At the end of the month you need to count all the food products in your restaurant and price them out. You should count everything in storage as well as the in-process inventory at the workstations.

To speed up the process you can split up the work between you and the bookkeeper. You can also adopt technology, such as **bar code readers,** that will count items and store them in the computer. Technology can also be set up to price items so that you don't have to do it by hand.

Once you have the total value of your month-end inventory, you need to calculate your monthly actual cost of food sold. The formula for this is:

	Opening (beginning) food inventory on 1st day of the month*
Plus:	**Food purchases during the month**
Less:	**Closing (ending) food inventory on last day of the month**
Equals:	**Actual cost of food used during the month**
Less:	**Cost of employee meals during the month**
Less:	**Other credit (such as manager's personal use) during the month**
Equals:	**Actual cost of food sold during the month**

*The opening inventory is equal to last month's closing inventory

This formula will give you a pretty good idea of the cost of food sold during the month as well as the cost of food used. These are critical figures. You need to know what they are so that you can make corrections if you find they are out of line.

Usually the cost of food used is greater than the cost of food sold; that is why you need to take into account things like employee meals and other relevant credits. You need to know, as accurately as possible, the actual cost of food sold to guests.

If you are pressed for time, you can ignore the employee meals and other credits. If you have a reasonable idea of what these credits are, if you can estimate them pretty well off the top of your head, you can merely take your actual cost of food used figure and reduce it by some percentage in order to come up with your actual cost of food sold. In addition, if you don't have a great deal of employee meal expense or other credits, it would make little difference if you ignored them altogether and treated the actual cost of food used as your actual cost of food sold.

If you take these kinds of short cuts, though, realize that you are going to suffer some inaccuracy. But unless you have a large support staff that can track everything very closely, it is not cost effective for you to do this if it means you have to neglect other important aspects of your business. You have to draw the line somewhere. You only have two hands. Your primary focus needs to be on filling the room with happy guests and enhancing the sales revenue figure. But you also have to maintain reasonable cost control. It's a delicate balancing act. We suppose if it were easy, anyone could do it.

After you calculate the actual cost of food sold, the next step is to divide it by the monthly food sales revenue in order to get your actual cost of food sold percentage for the month.

As an example, let's assume the following:

1. Your opening food inventory is $10,000.
2. You had food purchases during the month of $25,000.
3. Your ending food inventory is $7,500.
4. The cost of employee meals and other credit is $1,500.
5. The monthly food sales revenue is $100,000.

Actual cost of food sold
$$= \$10,000 + \$25,000 - \$7,500 - \$1,500 = \$26,000$$

Actual cost of food sold percentage
$$= \$26,000 \div \$100,000 = 0.26 = 26 \text{ percent}$$

Now that you have the cost percentage, the next step is to compare it to the expected cost percentage. After you've been in business for a short time, you get a pretty good feel for what the actual cost of food sold percentage should be. Eventually, a pattern of monthly cost percentages emerges that you can follow. If your current monthly cost percentage is consistent with this pattern, things are probably OK. If there is a wild swing, then you need to determine what's happening. Sometimes a big swing could mean nothing more than guests unexpectedly ordering more high-cost (or low-cost) items. Or, if the guests' ordering patterns haven't changed too much, then it could mean mistakes have been made somewhere in your operating procedures.

In our experience, if there is a big drop in your cost percentage, it means that more guests than expected are ordering the high-profit items. Recall that Chef Anthony Bourdain loved it when he sold tons of frites, because it meant his food cost was going way down. It's hard to lose money when people are paying $6.95 for something that costs you about $0.40 for its ingredients. When things like that happen, it gives you a lot of breathing room. That is why you have to focus on filling the room; the added sales revenue can cover up any minor mistakes.

Also in our experience, if there is an upward spike in your cost percentage, it usually means one of five things could be happening:

1. *There is something wrong with your calculations.* Did it ever happen that you called maintenance because the slicer wouldn't work? And the only thing the service tech did was to plug it in or reset the circuit breaker? When working with equipment, always check to see if it's plugged in. And when working with figures, before you proceed, always make sure that the formulas and/or the data are correct.

2. *You received a shipment of off-spec products.* The biggest potential problem is getting something that does not give you the expected yield. This can happen very easily if you're not careful and/or if you don't perform yield tests before buying from another vendor.

3. *There is extra production waste.* This happens when you have new employees, when you have interns, when you have a no-show/no-call and someone has to hurriedly take up the slack, or when people are working doubles and fatigue causes them to make more mistakes.

4. *The portion sizes are too big.* This can happen because of the reasons just mentioned. But many times servers and cooks overportion because they don't have the proper tools to work with. If, for instance, you don't have the right ladle in the ice cream toppings, the food servers are going to get frustrated. Chances are they'll end up giving guests too much (or too little, which is worse) and/or start spilling a lot of product on the counter.

5. Someone is ripping you off.

▨ BIWEEKLY PHYSICAL INVENTORY OF ALL BEVERAGE ALCOHOL ITEMS

If you are responsible for controlling the actual cost of beverage alcohol sold, our advice is to take a physical inventory about every two weeks. Beverage alcohol is expensive and people love to steal it, give it away to their friends, overpour, you name it. But if you track the products more closely, stealing will drop off to the point where you can live with it.

We like to outsource this type of inventory to a professional **inventory-taking service.** The one we're most familiar with is Bevinco, http://www.bevinco.com/. This firm has franchises all over the country that will come to your property, count everything, calculate your actual cost of beverage used and actual cost of beverage sold, and also tell you what your order sizes should be for your next period. As a bonus, and what we really love, is their ability to figure out, based on what you sold, how much sales revenue you should have collected. For instance, if you are supposed to get 10 drinks out of a bottle, and each drink sells for $5.00, then for every bottle missing, there should be 10 drinks rung up on the POS system (or 10 drink tickets in the lockbox) and $50.00 in the cash drawer. End of story.

You would think this type of service would be horribly expensive, but no way. One of our colleagues recently consulted with a local restaurant/lounge operation that was running a beverage cost of 45 to 50 percent. (Gee, you have to work pretty hard to run a number that high in the bar business.) Anyway, for about $250 per visit, the Bevinco franchisee essentially became this operation's bar manager. Think about it. A bar manager for about $16,000 a year. In this world of crumbling values, where can you get a deal like that? The best part: The cost percentage dropped like a rock, to the point where there was still a little stealing going on, but not enough to upset the owner.

▨ SHIFT-END INVENTORY OF YOUR MOST EXPENSIVE FOOD ITEMS

There are usually between 20 and 25 food items that make up at least 80 percent of your total food purchases. You need to protect these things every shift, every day. No exceptions.

Take a legal-size yellow pad and draw up five columns. On the left-hand side, list the food item; this will typically be the meat, fish, and poultry center-plate products. On the rest of the page insert column titles that note: (1) how many of each item was placed in service at each work station at the beginning of the shift; (2) how many were issued during the shift; (3) how many were left at the end of the shift; and (4) how many were used during the shift.

You will have a separate sheet of paper for each shift. At the end of the shift you take the amount that you started with at the beginning of the shift, add in whatever additional product was issued, and subtract what was left. This calculation will give you the usage of each item on the page. You then turn this piece of paper over to the bookkeeper, who will compare what was used to what was recorded in the POS system. There should be a perfect match. Each and every one of the items must be accounted for. Either they were sold, were rung up on the comp key, were voided, whatever. There must a legitimate reason for each one used. You must keep looking until you verify the usage; if you can't verify it, someone is stealing from you.

This type of daily calculation goes a long way toward protecting your inventory and preserving your target food cost percentage. In our opinion, when you combine it with the other two inventory procedures we recommend, you will have the best possible inventory control system for the least possible effort. It is the best possible option for the typical restaurant operation that does not have a huge support staff.

DIRECT CONTROL SYSTEM

Although it's important to crunch the numbers, an effective inventory control system also relies on your supervision and direction. That is, you should also incorporate a **direct control system** into your everyday activities. You have to be around. You have to walk the racetrack regularly. Did you know that there is a large, multiunit restaurant company that doesn't allow any chairs in the manager's office? Enough said. Get to work.

PURCHASING'S LINK TO EVERYTHING ELSE

We suppose that purchasing is involved in just about every restaurant activity, either directly or indirectly. It's kind of hard to get anything done unless there is enough "stuff" to work with.

THE FUTURE OF FOODSERVICE PROCUREMENT

Like you, we continually wonder what the future will be in this crazy industry of ours. Specifically, what changes in the purchasing activity can we expect in the coming years? To get some idea, we asked Mr. Reid A. Paul, editor of *Hospitality Technology,* to share his views. Here's what he had to say:

A few years ago, in the heyday of the technology boom, restaurant operators were told that the Internet would change their lives overnight. Experts insisted that the future of procurement had finally arrived, that e-procurement would become as ubiquitous as e-mail.

Times have changed and the hype has vanished. Most of the high-profile Internet-based procurement companies (also know as ASPs: application service providers) have come and gone; others have been purchased or developed a much lower profile. The idea and promise of online procurement did not die—it just grew more complicated.

This conclusion should hardly seem surprising. After all, if procurement were not complex, you undoubtedly would not be reading an entire textbook on the subject. What many of the early advocates for e-procurement forgot was that relationships between restaurants and foodservice distributors were frequently built on personal relationships, and on a host of other factors that are not easily translated to the Internet.

Still, despite the failure of the early e-procurement pioneers, that technology is now in use at many restaurants—typically in the hands of food distributors or the restaurants themselves. The Internet and e-procurement are slowly but steadily taking more significant roles in supply-chain management and procurement.

Espccially for multiunit restaurant operators, online tools help standardize procurement, and provide necessary checks on individual restaurant managers. These tools give corporate management greater control over procurement and play a large role in the efforts of restaurant companies to keep costs under control.

In fact, technology will continue to play an increasingly important role in procurement and supply-chain management. Although wireless Internet access in hotels and restaurants may get the most publicity, procurement and supply-chain management technologies will drive a growing number of restaurant companies to adopt wireless networks in the back of the house.

Already, many warehouses, consumer goods firms, and retail establishments have implemented wireless networks to improve inventory and supply-chain management control. These wireless networks allow workers to scan boxes, pallets, or individual items with a handheld device and wirelessly transmit the data to necessary systems.

In the world of retail, the momentum in this direction has been dramatically elevated by Walmart's declaration that all of its suppliers must implement **RFID (Radio Frequency Identification) tags** on each box or pallet. RFID tags—the same technology that allows electronic wireless toll payment in many states or the ExxonMobil SpeedPass wireless payment system—transmit data wirelessly to a sensor.

With the technology in place, Wal-Mart will be able to monitor its storage room automatically. As a result, Wal-Mart will be able to automate an increasing part of its procurement process with the data from the RFID-tagged shipments and improve its entire supply-chain management.

Not surprisingly, Wal-Mart and RFID technology have been afforded the same kind of attention and received the same kind of predictions that e-procurement received not long ago. The promise of RFID technology cannot be denied, but the reality of its implementation remains to be seen.

As the nation's largest retailer, Wal-Mart's leadership is significant, but the effect of this particular decision on foodservice procurement will most likely be muted. Retailers have utilized bar codes on their shipments for many years, while restaurant operators have struggled to do the same. For years, organizations like Efficient Foodservice Response (www.efr-central.com) have advocated the inclusion of bar codes on all foodservice shipments, with limited success.

Still, it is hard not to see the potential for restaurant procurement. Automated ordering and less time in the storage room or freezer easily translate into greater efficiency for restaurant operators. And *efficiency* is a word that all restaurant operators like.

As the experience of e-procurement vendors seems to indicate, restaurant operators are happiest, not in the forward lines of technological innovation, but following closely behind. In the study "Implementation Trends and Strategic Growth of Restaurant IT" (*Hospitality Technology,* University of Delaware and University of Nevada Las Vegas, 2003), 40 percent of restaurant operators indicated that their company was a "Close Follower" when it came to information technology. In contrast, only 18 percent considered their company a technology "Innovator or Leader." In the same study, while only 4 percent of the respondents indicated that more than half of their procurement was contracted online in 2002, 15 percent expect to utilize e-procurement at least half the time by 2004.

These may not be the monumental shifts predicted by the early e-procurement vendors, but they do indicate that restaurant operators are willing to closely follow new technology initiatives.

EQUIPMENT PURCHASING IN 2035?

We thought you might enjoy this short peek at what George E. Baggott, former chairman of CresCor—an international manufacturer of mobile foodservice equipment—thinks equipment, and equipment purchasing, will look like in the year 2035. Here are his insights:

The equipment world of the future: What is in store? What will change? Of course we cannot predict the future, but by looking at the trends of today we can catch a glimpse of what is to come.

Globalization. Foods of many lands. Foods from different cultures; equipment manufacturers will need to customize some of their products in order to accommodate specialized foods.

Kitchens. Space will be tight and rent will be at premium pricing; therefore equipment will need to perform multiple tasks. For example, a steaming unit will also act as a skillet and a combo-oven will have several new features.

Training. Because equipment will be multifunctional, training of chefs and employees will be crucial.

Technology. The Internet will be a key source of an equipment manufacturer's operation. Training, tracking of orders, usage, application, and communication between all parties will happen via the Web. We also must include Auto CAD, which will be able to take customers on a virtual tour of a new kitchen layout or give them an inside look at how the unit is assembled. Directions for installation will be made easy due to this technological breakthrough, as well as servicing of equipment.

Safety. All equipment will have to pass rigorous safety tests before being distributed. Stock pots will have to have a cool-down and dispensing feature. Holding ovens and refrigerators will be extremely sensitive in order to prevent food-borne illness. And hand-held tools, such as knives, will have a new design in order to protect the end user.

Trade shows. Networking and developing new relationships will continue to be extremely important. Shows will be done via the Internet, where new product designs can be shown and new deals made.

Customer service. Where would the world of purchasing be without the people who buy the equipment? Keeping these people happy now and in the future will make or break a business. Training, follow-up, servicing, and availability of parts will be crucial for success, as well as for gaining repeat business.

APPLY WHAT YOU'VE LEARNED

1. You have been running a full-service, fine-dining restaurant in a large metropolitan hotel with 17 outlets. Tomorrow is a meeting of all the hotel's chefs and outlet managers to review the monthly financials with the F & B director. As you are printing out your food costs, you begin to break out in a cold sweat. In a month, your restaurant's food cost jumped from 29.3 percent to 37.2 percent. It's 3:30 p.m., you've got an hour and a half before dinner service, and the meeting is at 8:00 in the morning, sharp. Oh, and you're working the line tonight and closing; it's your sous chef's night off. What could be going on at your restaurant to cause the food cost to jump?

2. Choose a menu from the establishment you work at, or one you are familiar with. Identify 20 to 25 food items that might be the most expensive items purchased. Write up a memo instructing all employees to conduct a shift-end inventory of these items so that you as chef can track them.

DISCUSSION QUESTIONS

1. Explain the rules of thumb that chefs follow to know how much inventory to keep on hand.

2. Name four storage problems that insufficient space and inadequate equipment can cause.

3. Are there any advantages to tight storage?

4. Name five methods that can be used to reduce spoilage and stealing.

5. Describe a typical physical inventory procedure.

6. How is the actual cost of food sold calculated?

7. How is the actual cost of food sold percentage calculated?

8. You are the chef/owner of an upscale catering company in South Beach. Last month, you increased the prices on your menus with no loss in business, but wonder how the increased revenue changed your actual cost of food sold percentage. Assume the following:

☑ Your opening food inventory is $15,000

☑ You had food purchases during the month of $38,000

☑ Your ending food inventory is $17,500

☑ The cost of employee meals and other credit is $2,200

☑ The monthly food sales revenue is $180,000

Calculate the actual cost of food sold and the actual cost of food sold percentage.

9. What are steward sales? Explain some of their pros and cons.

10. Describe the first four things to check in the receiving process.

11. What are some potential disadvantages of entering orders on vendors' Web sites?

12. What is a kickback?

13. When a computerized inventory file is kept for purchasing, what three things are typically updated after a shipment?

14. What is a stock requisition? What advantages does it offer to the restaurant operation?

15. What are some of the problems associated with adding vendors without investigating them first?

16. In your work experience, what purchasing security problems have you encountered or heard about?

RESOURCES

CITY & STA

ZIP CODE

CITY & STATE

TERMS

HOW SHIPPED

UNIT PRICE

DATE REQUIRED

DESCRIPTION

UNIT

Here is a brief listing of some of the major resources designed to help you prepare the appropriate, relevant specifications for the food and beverage products you typically order for your restaurant.

FRESH PRODUCE
Florida Fruit & Vegetable Association
    http://www.ffva.com/
Produce Marketing Association
    http://www.pma.com/
United Fresh Fruit and Vegetable Association
    http://www.uffva.org/
United States Department of Agriculture (USDA)
    http://www.usda.gov/

GROCERIES
The Canned Vegetable Council
    http://www.cannedvegies.org/
National Frozen & Refrigerated Foods Association
    http://www.nfraweb.org/
United States Department of Agriculture (USDA)
    http://www.usda.gov/

DAIRY
International Dairy Foods Association
    http://www.idfa.org/
Wisconsin Specialty Cheese Institute
    http://www.wisspecialcheese.org/
United States Department of Agriculture (USDA)
    http://www.usda.gov/

EGGS
American Egg Board
    http://www.aeb.org/
United Egg Association
    http://www.unitedegg.org/

POULTRY
The American Meat Institute
    http://www.meatami.com/

National Poultry and Food Distributors Association
http://www.npfda.org/
National Turkey Federation
http://www.eatturkey.org/
North American Meat Processors Association
http://www.namp.com/
United States Department of Agriculture (USDA)
http://www.usda.gov/

FISH
The American Seafood Distributors Association
http://www.freetradeinseafood.org/
National Fisheries Institute
http://www.nfi.org/
Seafood Business
http://www.seafoodbusiness.com/
Aquaculture Network Information Center
http://www.aquanic.org/
National Marine Fisheries Service
http://www.nmfs.noaa.gov/

MEAT
The American Meat Institute
http://www.meatami.com/
National Cattlemen's Beef Association
http://www.beef.org/
North American Meat Processors Association
http://www.namp.com/
United States Department of Agriculture (USDA)
http://www.usda.gov/

BEVERAGE ALCOHOL AND NONALCOHOLIC BEVERAGES
American Beverage Institute
http://www.abionline.org/
The Beer Institute
http://www.beerinstitute.org/
The Distilled Spirits Council of the United States
http://www.discus.org/
The Wine Institute
http://www.wineinstitute.org/

Wine and Spirits Wholesalers of America
  http://www.wswa.org/
National Soft Drink Association
  http://www.nsda.org/
Bottled Water Web
  http://www.bottledwaterweb.com/

ZIP CODE

PURCHASING
TERMINOLOGY

ZIP CODE

CITY & STATE

TERMS

UNIT PRICE

HOW SHIPPED

DATE REQUIRED

DESCRIPTION

UNIT

Accepting a delivery. Occurs when a receiving agent is satisfied that the delivered merchandise meets the company's standards. Once the shipment is accepted, the receiving agent normally signs a copy of the invoice accompanying the delivery.

Accredited Purchasing Practitioner. Buyers holding this certification have demonstrated a certain level of purchasing knowledge and experience.

Actual cost of food sold. Equal to the actual cost of food used (consumed), less credits for things like the cost of employee meals and food for the manager's personal use.

Actual cost of food used (consumed). Equal to the opening food inventory plus food purchases minus the closing food inventory.

Actual inventory value. The value of the physical inventory, determined by pricing each item in that inventory and then computing the total.

Add-on capability. Feature that allows retrofitting in the future. Especially important when purchasing equipment that may need to be modified as the business grows.

Additives. Chemicals added or used to upgrade product quality and/or help product resist spoilage.

Age of bird at time of slaughter. Characteristic that affects the flavor, tenderness, and other culinary characteristics of poultry.

Aggregate buying group. Another term for co-op buying.

Aggregate purchasing company. Another term for buying club.

Alcohol Beverage Commission (ABC). A liquor control authority that regulates the sale and purchase of beverage alcohol.

Allocation. Term used in the wine business. A wine distributor determines how much of the product you are allowed to purchase. Done so that all restaurants have a chance at buying at least some of it.

Approved-payee list. A list of all persons and companies that are allowed to receive any sort of payment from you. An excellent security precaution.

Approved substitute. A product that a buyer can purchase in lieu of the typical one that is normally purchased.

Approved-supplier list. A list of all vendors who buyers are allowed to purchase from. An excellent security precaution.

Approximate waste percentage. The amount of product loss expressed as a percentage of its original amount. It is calculated by dividing the unusable amount of product by its original amount, and multiplying by 100.

Aquaculture. Another term for fish farming. Fish are grown and harvested under controlled conditions.

Aseptic packaging. A form of Controlled Atmosphere Packaging (CAP). Sterile foods are placed in an air-tight, sterilized package. The package contains a hygienic environment that prolongs shelf life and makes the foods shelf stable.

As-is, where-is condition. Buying a product, such as a used piece of equipment, in its current condition. There are usually no guarantees. In addition, the buyer is usually responsible for the cost of packing up the product and having it delivered.

As-purchased (AP) price. Price charged by the vendor.

As-purchased (AP) weight. The original weight of an item purchased.

As-served cost. Another term for edible-portion (EP) cost.

As-used cost. Another term for edible-portion (EP) cost.

Auditing the inventory sales. Process whereby a supervisor or manager compares inventory that has been used in production to the sales records. Ideally, the amount missing would be recorded as sold to customers.

Average inventory. The sum of opening inventory and closing inventory for a period, divided by 2.

B2B e-commerce. Online interaction between businesses. Typically involves the sale and purchase of merchandise or services.

B2C e-commerce. Online interaction between businesses and consumers. Typically involves the sale and purchase of merchandise and services.

Backdoor selling. This happens when a sales rep bypasses the regular buyer and goes to some other employee, such as the lead line cook, to make a sales pitch. The cook then exerts pressure on the buyer to make the purchase.

Background check (investigation). Researching someone's, or some company's, history, checking for things such as reliability, unethical behavior, criminal convictions, and so forth. Alternately, another term for pre-employment screening.

Backhaul. Occurs when a driver delivers a shipment to a hospitality operation and then refills the empty truck with items (such as recyclable materials) that need to be delivered to another location. The purpose is to gain maximum efficiency by seeing to it that the truck is always full when it is on the road.

Back order. When your shipment is incomplete because the vendor did not have the item in stock. The invoice will state that the item is back ordered. You will receive it later.

Bag-in-the-box container. An aseptic package. Bulk product, such as wine or soda pop syrup, is packed in a plastic liner and then placed into a cardboard box. The container may also serve as the dispensing unit.

Bar code. A computerized label attached to most food packages. The information on the bars can be read by the computer. It can be used to track inventory amounts and values.

Bar code element. The lines and spaces on a bar code label.

Bar code reader. Device used to read labels that contain bar code elements.

Bargaining power. Another term for purchasing power.

Barter. The practice of trading your products or services for something you need. Intended to reduce your out-of-pocket expense.

Barter group. A group of businesses that wish to barter for products and services and use trade dollars instead of cash money to get what they need. The group is organized and administered by a third party and a fee is usually assessed each participant whenever they make a deal. The opposite of "direct" bartering, whereby two or more persons get together on their own to make a deal.

Beginning inventory. Amount of products available for sale at the beginning of an accounting period.

Best-if-consumed-by date. Another term for pull date.

Best-if-used-by date. Another term for pull date.

Bid. The AP price a vendor is willing to charge buyers for a product or service.

Bid buying. When buyers shop around seeking current purchase prices from vendors. The vendors are asked to quote, or bid, the prices they will charge. Intended to give the buyer competitive pricing information that will allow him or her to get the best possible value.

Bill of lading. A document that represents title to the goods received.

Bill-paying service. An outside company that uses a buyer's company's money to pay for products or services the buyer purchases. Bills are typically paid automatically by accessing the buyer's company's bank account(s). The service is typically used in order to reduce the buyer's company's administrative expenses and to increase efficiency.

Bin card. A perpetual inventory record. It includes all items delivered to the restaurant's stock room, all items issued out of the stock room, all items returned to the stock room, and the current balance of all items held in the stock room.

Blanket order. Purchase order that contains several different products.

Blanket-order discount. Another term for volume discount.

Blind date. Similar to pull date. The difference is that a blind date is written in code that the average buyer may not understand, whereas the pull date is written in plain language.

Blind receiving. When the invoice accompanying a delivery contains only the names of the items delivered. Quantity and price information is missing. The receiving clerk is required to count everything and record it. An expensive way of controlling the receiving clerk's work.

Blowout sale. Usually refers to merchandise that is old, defective, or discontinued sold at a huge discount.

Bonding. An insurance policy covering cash-handling employees. May also refer to a performance bond, which is insurance taken out by a construction contractor that guarantees work will be done by a certain date or else the client will collect damages.

Bottom-line, firm-price purchasing. The buyer focuses on the total dollar amount of a purchase instead of on each item's AP price. If shopping around, the buyer will not pick and choose among several vendors. He or she will buy from the one that quotes the lowest total dollar amount of the entire purchase and will not purchase anything from the other competing vendors. The opposite of line-item purchasing.

Brand incentive. Another term for proprietary brand discount.

Brand name. Indication of product quality. A typical selection factor for purchased items, especially when purchasing beverage alcohol.

Break point. The point at which a vendor will accept a lower price. For instance, if you buy from 1 to 50 cases, the AP price may be $5.00 per case. But if you purchase more than 50 cases, the AP price may be $4.75 per case. In this example, the break point is 50.

Broad view of purchasing. Where the buyer attempts to consider every aspect of purchasing and not just the fundamental tasks, such as ordering and supplier selection. For instance, the buyer might consider how a purchase of, say, a convenience food item might impact the production and service styles in a restaurant operation.

Broadline distributor. Intermediary that distributes food, non-food supplies, and equipment.

Broadliner. Another term for broadline distributor.

Broken case. Refers to the purchase of less than one case. The vendor is willing to break open a case and sell you only part of it. Few vendors will do this for you.

Broker. An agent who represents one or more manufacturers. A broker does not buy or resell products. His or her job is to promote products to potential buyers. A broker usually represents manufacturers that do not employ their own sales forces.

Budget. A realistic statement of management's goals and objectives, expressed in financial terms.

Bulk pack. The product is packed in a very large package. The AP price per unit is usually less than smaller packages, and much less than single-serve packages.

Busted case. Another term for broken case.

Butcher test. Another term for yield test. Typically refers to a yield test performed on meat, fish, and poultry products.

Buy-and-hold purchasing. Refers to purchasing and taking delivery of a huge amount of product during the traditional time(s) of the year when AP prices are typically at their lowest and the supply of the product is typically at its highest peak.

Buyer fact sheets. Another term for buyer profiles.

Buyer pricing. This method will significantly increase your cost of goods sold. Occurs whenever a buyer does not have a clear-cut specification; the vendor helps the buyer determine what he or she needs. Will also occur whenever you engage in panic buying.

Buyer profiles. Vendor files that contain information about current and potential customers. Typically used by sales reps to help them prepare the best possible sales presentations.

Buying club. A type of co-op purchasing. Instead of co-op members organizing and administering their own co-op they join a buying club that, for a fee, streamlines the process and makes it more efficient.

Buying plan. Overall purchasing strategy. Includes reasons why it was selected, and relevant policies and procedures needed to carry it out successfully.

Buying power. Another term for purchasing power.

Buying service. Another term for buying club.

Buyout policy. Vendors' willingness to purchase from a customer, a competitor's products, so that the customer can immediately begin purchasing similar products from them.

Buyout sale. Another term for blowout sale.

Call brand. Refers to the type of drink served to guests when they order a specific brand of beverage alcohol.

Call sheet buying. Used when shopping around on a day-to-day basis. The buyer contacts several purveyors seeking their AP price quotes. He or she then purchases from the one offering the lowest AP price.

Can-cutting test. Examining the characteristics of two or more similar products in order to determine which one represents the best value. Alternately, an examination of all relevant characteristics of a product the buyer is thinking about purchasing.

Carrying cost. Expenses, such as insurance, security, and spoilage, associated with holding inventory in storage.

Case price per unit. Equal to the AP price for one case ÷ number of units per case. For instance, if you pay $12.00 for a six-can case of canned tomatoes, the case price is $2.00 per can. If a vendor is willing to sell you less than one case, but charges you only $2.00 per can, he or she is charging the case price and not a premium price for a broken (busted) case.

Cash-and-carry buying. Another term for will-call buying.

Cash discount. An award for prompt payment, for paying in advance of the delivery, or using a cash-on-delivery (COD) bill-paying procedure.

Cash-on-delivery (COD). Paying for a shipment when it is delivered. Payment may be in cash, check, credit card, debit card, or other acceptable means.

Cash rebate. Occurs when a vendor charges the full AP price for an item, but later on, after you provide proof-of-purchase documentation, he or she will send you a check for a small amount of money, or will credit this amount to your account.

Catalog house. A very small equipment dealer that carries no inventory, or very little inventory, in stock. Buyers select items from one or more catalogs, and the dealer handles the ordering, delivery, setup, installation, and so forth.

Catch weight. The approximate weight in a case of product. Used when it is not possible to specify an exact weight. For instance, if you purchase a case of whole, fresh fish, you usually cannot specify the exact total weight of all pieces, but you can ask for an approximate total weight of the case.

Cello pack. Products completely surrounded by clear plastic film. Typical packing procedure for things like ready-to-serve salad greens. Also commonly used as an inner wrap. For instance, if you purchase a 5-pound box of frozen fish fillets, usually there will be six cello-wrapped packages, each containing approximately two to four pieces of fish.

Cello wrap. Another term for cello pack.

Cell pack. Products are layered in a cardboard or plastic sheet that has depressions in it so that the items sit in them and do not touch each other. Typically used to pack high-quality fresh fruit.

Central distribution center. A large warehouse owned by a multiunit restaurant company that orders merchandise directly from the manufacturers, takes delivery, stocks the merchandise, and delivers it to company-affiliated restaurant units in the area.

Certified Purchasing Manager (CPM). Indication that the person who holds this designation has achieved a certain level of purchasing knowledge and experience.

Change order. Used if a buyer wishes to alter a purchase order that was recently placed with a vendor. May be a written document, or it could be accomplished with a phone call or e-mail.

Chemical standards. The amount and/or type of additives a buyer is willing to accept in purchased products.

Cherry-picking. See line-item purchasing.

Child nutrition (CN) label. Indicates that the products in the container conform to the nutritional requirements of the United States Department of Agriculture (USDA). An important consideration for school foodservice buyers.

Chill pack. A preservation method, whereby the temperature is held at approximately 28°F to 29°F, just above the product's freezing point. Usually done for fresh meat and poultry. Intended to increase the product's shelf life.

Closeout sale. Another term for blowout sale.

Closing inventory. Another term for ending inventory.

Code compliance. Following the laws and regulations of a governing body. Term typically used to refer to compliance with building, equipment, and health codes.

Comminuting. Process of reducing a substance into smaller, random-shaped pieces. Typical method used to produce things like processed chicken patties.

Commissary. Similar to a central distribution center. The major difference is that at a commissary, raw foods are processed into finished products, which is not the case in a central distribution center. Could be considered a restaurant company's personal convenience-food-processing plant.

Commodity. A basic, raw food ingredient. It is considered by buyers to be the same, regardless of which vendor sells it. For instance, all-purpose flour is oftentimes considered a commodity product, whereby any manufacturer's product is acceptable.

Common can sizes. Containers typically used in the foodservice industry. The most common size is the No. 10 can.

Common carrier. An independent delivery service hired by the vendor to deliver goods to the restaurant operation. UPS is an example of a common carrier.

Communal buying. Another term for co-op buying.

Competitive bid. Another term for bid.

Consignment sale. Allows the buyer to pay a vendor for a purchase after the buyer's company has sold the merchandise to its customers.

Consistency. Continually providing the same quality and service over the long term. Important vendor selection factor.

Consortium buying. Another term for co-op buying.

Contract. Voluntary and legal agreement, by competent parties, to do or not do something. In almost every case it must be a written agreement in order to be legally enforceable.

Contract house. Another term for buying club.

Control. Systems and procedures used by managers to ensure that the actual costs of doing business are consistent with the expected (or *budgeted* or *theoretical*) costs.

Control documents. Computerized and/or noncomputerized records that track the receipt and disbursement of company assets. Typically used to control a company's working capital assets, such as inventory and cash.

Control state. A state that sells beverage alcohol. It is the only purveyor of beverage alcohol in that state.

Controlled atmosphere packaging (CAP). Process that involves placing a food or beverage item in a package, removing existing gases by creating a vacuum, and introducing a specially formulated mixture of gasses intended to enhance the product's shelf life.

Controlled atmosphere storage. Similar to controlled atmosphere packaging (CAP). Refers to a controlled atmosphere that exists in other types of storage environments, such as controlled atmosphere warehouses.

Controlled brand. Products produced by a company that typically offers only one level of quality (usually a high quality). The company controls all aspects of production and distribution.

Convenience food. A food that has been processed by a manufacturer to change its form and/or taste. It usually requires very little handling in the restaurant kitchen. It may be ready to use or ready to serve.

Conversion weight. Another term for edible yield.

Co-op buying. The banding together of several small operators in order to consolidate their buying power.

Correct order size. The order size that minimizes the ordering costs, carrying costs, and stockout costs.

Correct order time. The order time that minimizes the ordering costs, carrying costs, and stockout costs.

Cost control. See control.

Cost limitation. Constraint that indicates the maximum amount of money a buyer can pay for a product or service.

Cost of goods sold (COGS). See actual cost of food sold.

Cost of paying too early. The loss of interest income that could have been collected if the cash were invested between the time the bill was paid early and the time it had to be paid.

Cost of paying too late. Includes things such as damage to a company's credit rating, late fee charges, and being required to pay COD for future purchases.

Cost per servable pound. Information needed to calculate standard portion costs, determined by dividing the AP price by the yield percentage (expressed as a decimal).

Cost percentage. The ratio of cost to sales revenue, expressed as a percentage.

Cost-plus buying. The AP price the buyer pays is equal to the vendor's cost of the product plus an agreed-upon profit markup.

Count. The number of pieces in a container. Alternately, the number of smaller containers in a larger container.

Coupon refund. Another term for cash rebate.

Credit control. Refers to government agencies dictating the credit terms that can be extended to buyers. This type of control is fairly common in the dairy and beverage alcohol distribution channels.

Credit memo. A note sent to the vender requesting credit because all or part of a shipment was unacceptable.

Credit period. The amount of time a borrower has before a bill must be paid.

Credit rating. Another term for credit score.

Credit risk. The probability that a borrower will not pay.

Credit score. A system that is used to calculate a number (i.e., *score*) that creditors (e.g., vendors) then use to help determine whether to give a buyer credit. Information about the buyer's company and its credit experiences, such as bill-paying history, outstanding debt, and so forth, is collected and analyzed to compute the score. The score is typically computed by a credit reporting agency, such as Equifax, Experian, and TransUnion.

Credit slip. When a shipment, or partial shipment, is unsatisfactory, the driver will give one of these to the receiving clerk, signifying the amount of credit that will be applied to the restaurant's account. It eliminates the need for the restaurant to prepare a credit memo.

Credit terms. The type and amount of financing a vendor will provide, along with the prescribed type of bill-paying procedure that must be followed. Also included are things such as a description of late fees, penalties, and so forth.

Critical item inventory. A list of the restaurant's most expensive ingredients kept in stock. They are tightly controlled by tracking their daily usage.

Critical item inventory analysis. Reconciling the critical item inventory daily usage with the daily sales recorded in the POS system. Discrepancies between what was used and what was sold must be resolved.

Cryovac. The company that pioneered shrink-wrap technology.

Cryovac aging. Another term for wet aging.

Cryovac-packed. A form of shrink wrap.

Custom packaging. Packing products in a specific way with a specific type of packaging material. The packaging typically includes the buyer's company logo.

Customized FFE. FFE items specially made to fit a buyer's unique needs. Typically manufactured on a made-to-order basis.

Cutting. Another term for can-cutting test.

Daily bid buying. Another term for call sheet buying.

Daily quotation buying. Another term for call sheet buying.

Daisy chain. When vendors sell products back and forth among themselves. Each time the product is "sold," its price is increased. Done in an attempt to inflate artificially the price of products.

Dead stock. Obsolete or discontinued stock items no longer in regular use due to menu or service changes.

Dead weight. Another term for tare weight.

Decay allowance. The expected amount of a purchased product that will be unusable, yet will be acceptable to the buyer when it is shipped to the restaurant. Typical situation involves the purchase of fresh produce where the buyer may expect, and accept, a few broken and/or spoiled pieces in the lot.

Default risk. Another term for credit risk.

Delivery cost. The expense incurred in order to move products from one location to another.

Delivery schedule. Purveyor's planned shipping times and dates.

Delivery ticket. Written receipt summarizing what was ordered and delivered. It is typically written up by route salespersons when they are finished restocking the restaurant. Similar to an invoice.

Demonstration (demo) model. FFE used by the purveyor or manufacturer for display purposes. Usually can be purchased at a discount.

Deposit. Money, or other asset, used to ensure that future products or services will be provided. Alternately, money, or other asset, used to ensure that returnable items, such as reusable packing crates, will be returned to the vendor.

Derived demand. Refers to the notion that a buyer's demand for certain products and/or services is contingent on the needs and desires of the customers the buyer's company serves.

Direct bartering. When two persons trade between themselves. They do not trade through a barter group.

Direct buying. Bypassing intermediaries and purchasing directly from the manufacturer.

Direct control system. A system that does not rely on number crunching and paperwork. It relies on the supervisor's presence, supervision, and personal direction.

Direct purchase. Refers to a purchased product (usually a perishable food) that, once received, will bypass the main storage facility, go straight to production, and be charged to cost on the day it's received. A perishable food item, such as fresh pastry, is an example of a direct purchase.

Directs. Another term for direct purchases.

Discount operation. Another term for storefront dealer.

Disintermediation. Occurs when manufacturers bypass intermediaries and sell to the restaurant operators directly.

Distributor. Another term for vendor.

Distributor sales rep (DSR). Person employed by a vendor to sell products and provide support functions to restaurant operators.

Distribution channel. The people, organizations, and procedures involved in producing and delivering products and services from manufacturers to ultimate consumers.

Distribution list. Directory of people, groups, and/or businesses that are eligible to receive products and/or services.

Downtime. The amount of time a piece of equipment or a facility is out of service.

Dot system. Color-coded, stick-on dots (usually a different color for each day) usually attached to inventories when they are received. They have enough blank space to pencil in dates, times, AP prices, and other pertinent information.

Drained weight. When purchasing canned goods, this refers to the weight of the product less its juice (or other packing medium). It is computed by draining the product in a specific sieve for a certain amount of time. Sometimes referred to as the edible weight, usable weight, or servable weight.

Drawn fish. Whole fish that has been eviscerated, i.e., the entrails have been removed.

Dressed fish. A completely clean fish; can be cooked as is or processed into steaks, fillets, portions, etc.

Drink fee. A modest charge deducted from an employee's paycheck. The employee is then allowed to consume unlimited amounts of nonalcoholic beverages while on the job.

Drop shipment. Typical shipping procedure used when buying direct. The shipment is delivered to the back door of the restaurant, usually by a common carrier.

Drop-size discount. Another term for volume discount.

Drop-size incentive. Another term for drop-size discount.

Due bill. Another term for trade-out.

E-commerce. Refers to business transactions done electronically.

Economical packaging. Packing methods and packaging materials used that will reduce overall product costs.

Economic value. Represents the increase in AP price that occurs as a product journeys through the distribution channel. For example, 10 pounds of preportioned steak is more valuable, and more expensive, than 10 pounds of meat that has to be processed further in a restaurant's kitchen.

Edible byproducts. Trimmings of food items, such as meat and seafood that can be processed into another type of menu item. For instance, meat trimmings left over from cutting steaks may be processed into hamburgers.

Edible-portion (EP) cost. Equal to the AP price per portion divided by its edible yield percentage.

Edible-portion (EP) weight. Difference between the original weight of a product and the production loss incurred after preparing it for service to guests.

Edible yield. Another term for yield.

Edible yield percentage. Another term for yield percentage.

Efficiency food. Another term for convenience food.

Efficient Foodservice Response (EFR). Processes and procedures used by food distributors to help reduce overall cost and time needed to distribute food products to buyers in the foodservice industry.

Electronic co-op. Another term for buying club.

Electronic marketplace. An Internet application allowing buyers to locate vendors, research products and services, solicit competitive bids, and place orders electronically.

Electronic procurement. Ordering products and services from various purveyors over the Internet. Alternately, ordering these things from a particular vendor who provides proprietary software to the buyer, who is then allowed to enter the vendor's electronic system.

Element. Another term for bar code element.

E-marketplace. Another term for electronic marketplace.

Ending inventory. Amount of product on hand at the end of an accounting period.

Endorsement. Testimonial by an independent agency or person, expressing approval and satisfaction with a company's product or service.

End-user services. Support functions provided to buyers by vendors. Includes everything except the sales effort, which is provided by an independent broker.

Environmentally safe packaging. Packaging materials that do not harm the natural surroundings during their production, use, and disposal.

E-procurement application. Software that allows customers to select and purchase products over the Internet.

Equal or better. Tells the vendor that the buyer will accept a substitute item if it is the same, or better, quality.

Equal-to-facing layer. Refers to the fact that when you purchase layered merchandise, you want all the layers to look just like the top (facing) one. You don't want the junk hidden underneath the facing layer.

Equipment dealer. Company that purchases equipment from a manufacturer and resells it to restaurant buyers.

Equipment program. Process whereby a purveyor allows you the free use of equipment if you purchase other products. For instance, if you purchase all your coffees and teas from a vendor, it may offer you the free use of the brewing and serving equipment. In some cases there may be a nominal surcharge for the equipment; it's not always free.

E-sourcing. Electronic form of sourcing. Allows buyers to identify, qualify, and select vendors over the Internet.

Exchange bartering. Another term for barter.

Exclusive dealing. Occurs when a salesperson allows a buyer to purchase the brands he or she carries, only if the buyer agrees to purchase no competing brands from other vendors. An illegal practice.

Exclusive distributor. A vendor who has the exclusive right to sell a particular product or product line. For instance, if you want Sara Lee brand pastries, there may be only one vendor in your area that sells it; this eliminates your ability to shop around for these items.

Exclusive selling. Another term for exclusive distributor.

Exclusive territory. The geographical area in which an exclusive distributor is allowed to operate as the sole vendor of certain brands of merchandise.

Executive steward. Oversees cleaning crews. Typically also has purchasing responsibilities for things such as soaps, chemicals, and other cleaning supplies. May also control the china, glass, and silver inventories.

Expediting. To move shipments through the distribution channel at an accelerated rate. Alternately, the process used in a kitchen (or bar) to coordinate the orders from food servers (or cocktail servers) to cooks (or bartenders) to ensure efficiency and timeliness.

Expiration date. Another term for pull date.

Extended price. Equal to the AP price per unit times the number of units purchased.

Farmers' market. Area where local farmers, growers, and other merchants come together to sell their own products directly to consumers.

FFE. Acronym for furniture, fixtures, and equipment.

Fictitious invoice. Fraudulent bill sent to a company with the hope that the company will not check it closely and just pay it, along with all the other bills it receives. May be part of a kickback scheme.

Field inspector. A person hired by a company to inspect products before they are shipped to the company. Typically done when purchasing large amounts of fresh produce directly from the farmer.

Field run. Refers to fresh produce items that have not been graded. They may be low-quality items intended to be used by food processors to make things such as juice, jam, jelly, and so forth.

FIFO. Stands for first-in, first-out. A method of stock rotation used to ensure that older products are used first.

Fill rate. An important vendor selection factor. Equal to the amount of items delivered ÷ the amount of items ordered, times 100. For instance, if you ordered 10 items and the vendor delivered only 9, the fill rate is 90% (9 ÷ 10 × 100). A fill rate less than 100% indicates that the vendor is out of some items and has to back order you.

First-generation convenience food. Value-added product that was one of the first convenience foods on the market. It has been available for many years. May be less expensive than its fresh counterpart. An example is frozen orange juice.

Fixed-bid buying. Shopping around and soliciting competitive bids for long-term contracts.

Fixed-price contract. Contract that does not allow price fluctuations.

Flaked and reformed food product. Item typically made from edible byproducts and other foods. It is formed to resemble a whole product. An example would be a chicken patty made from odd scraps of chicken meat formed and shaped to look like a whole piece.

Flat. Refers to one layer of a product. Term typically used in the fresh produce trade.

Food buyer. Another term for steward.

Food cost. See actual cost of food sold.

Food cost percentage. Equal to the actual cost of food sold divided by food sales revenue, times 100.

Food distributor. Another term for vendor.

Foodservice Purchasing Managers (FPM) Executive Study Group. Group of foodservice purchasing professionals.

Forecasting. An attempt to predict the future. Current and historical information is used to estimate what might happen over the near or long term.

Forklift discount. A price reduction if you agree to unload your own shipments instead of requiring the drivers to do the unloading.

Form value. An economic value that refers to the degree of processing, or lack thereof, a product has when you purchase it. When a product has more form (i.e., convenience), typically the AP price will be higher.

Forward buying. When a buyer purchases a large amount of product (for example, a three-month supply) and takes delivery of the entire shipment.

Franchise. A business form where the owner (franchisor) allows others (franchisees) to use his or her operating procedures, name, and so forth, for a fee.

Free alongside ship (FAS). Similar to free on board (FOB), but typically a more complicated process. Occurs, for example, when a buyer purchases a product from a vendor located across the sea. The vendor will place the product on the ship, and from that point on, the buyer's company is responsible for it. When the ship docks, the buyer will have to ensure that another vehicle is standing by ready to take it from the dock to the buyer's establishment. Or, the vehicle may have to bring the product to a train, and when the train arrives in the buyer's city, the buyer will have to arrange for another vehicle to transport the product to the buyer's establishment.

Free on board (FOB). When buyers purchase merchandise, but have to arrange for their own delivery. The vendor will place the merchandise on the buyer's vehicle or a common carrier at no additional charge (i.e., free on board), but the buyer is then responsible for the merchandise and the cost of transportation from that point on.

Free sample. Part of the marketing strategy used by vendors to sell products. Buyers are allowed to test a product in their own facility without having to pay for it.

Freezer burn. The loss of moisture from a food product while it is held in frozen storage. Typically causes dry (i.e., burned) spots on the product, as well as an unpleasant odor.

Freight-damaged discount. Offered if you are willing to accept an item that was damaged in shipping. The damage usually does not inhibit the product's usefulness; it is typically cosmetic.

Freshness date. Another term for pull date.

Full-line distributor. A vendor that provides food products and nonfood supplies.

Full-service dealer. FFE vendor that typically carries a full line of inventory and is able to provide all end-user services.

Gas-flushed pack. A type of controlled atmosphere packaging (CAP).

Generic brand. The package label typically does not refer directly to the company that processed the item. Rather, the label generally highlights only the name of the item while downplaying other information. Its quality is very unpredictable. Typically, it is low-quality merchandise that is sold to economy-minded buyers.

Genetically altered food. Food modified by bioengineering techniques. Typically done to enhance flavor, appearance, and/or uniformity of size, and to increase shelf life.

Gifts from suppliers. Controversial subject in the purchasing profession. Occurs when the buyer receives an item of personal gain from vendors in appreciation for buying their products. Buyers are usually forbidden from accepting any significant personal gift. A valuable gift could be interpreted as a kickback.

Glaze. A thin coating of ice applied to frozen products, such as boneless, skinless chicken breasts. Done to provide protection from freezer burn.

Going-out-of-business sale. Held to dispose of all remaining inventory and, in some cases, of all the existing FFE. Everything is typically sold at heavily discounted prices.

Goods received without invoice slip. Created by the receiving agent to record a shipment when no invoice or delivery document accompanies the shipment. Without a record of shipments received, a hospitality operation wouldn't be able to calculate actual costs.

Grading factors. Characteristics of food or beverage products examined by grading inspectors. Used to judge and rank products.

Gross weight. Weight of product plus the tare weight.

Group purchasing organization (GPO). Another term for buying club.

Guarantee. May be expressed or implied. (1) Assurance that a product or service will be provided. (2) Assurance that a product or service will meet certain specifications. (3) Assurance that a product or service will be acceptable for a specified period of time or amount of use. (4) Assurance that parts and/or repairs needed during a specified time period will be paid for by the vendor.

Hazard Analysis Critical Control Point system (HACCP). Process used by food manufacturers and others in the foodservice industry to ensure food safety. It identifies the areas at which foods are most susceptible to contamination and recommends procedures that can be used to prevent it from occurring.

Heavy equipment dealer. Specializes in handling large equipment installations. Carries inventory. Usually involved in the layout and design of new hospitality properties or major renovations.

Heavy pack. Packing product with very little added juice or water.

Holding court. Refers to a buyer analyzing several competing products while the competing vendors are in attendance.

House account. Term used by a vendor to identify a very loyal customer. A customer who continually buys from a vendor and is not interested in buying from any other vendors.

House brand. Another term for well brand. Alternately, another term for proprietary brand.

House wine. Refers to the well brand of wine used when customers ordering wine do not specify a particular brand name.

HRI Meat Price Report. Weekly guide of prices charged by U.S. meat processors.

Hydroponics. Method of growing plants in nutrient-rich water instead of chemically treated soil.

Hyperlinks. Permits Web surfers to select a word or image and connect to more information about that topic.

Hypoallergenic food. Food that has a decreased tendency to provoke an allergic reaction in persons who consume it.

Ice pack. Foods packed in crushed ice. Intended to increase shelf life. A typical packing procedure used for things like fresh chickens and fish.

Ice spot. A dry spot on a food product that has been previously frozen. An indication that an item that is thought to be fresh has actually been frozen, thawed, and passed off as fresh.

Identification code (ID). Product information read by a bar code reader. The information is based on a standard that associates various details with that product. The most commonly used standard is the Universal Product Code (UPC). However, other standards, such as EAN, Codabar, and Code 128, are also in use.

Illegal rebate. Another term for kickback.

Imitation meat product. Product made from nonmeat ingredients, such as fish or chicken. Intended to have many of the same culinary characteristics as if it were made with the real meat. Typically the product costs less than the real thing. It may also be more nutritious than the real thing.

Importer-wholesaler. Intermediary in the beverage alcohol distribution channel. Responsible for importing products into the United States, as well as into each state and local municipality. Also responsible for distribution to retail establishments, such as bars, restaurants, and liquor stores.

IMPS/NAMP number. Another term for Institutional Meat Purchase Specification (IMPS) number.

Impulse buy. A purchase made on the spur-of-the-moment. No prior analysis is made.

Individually quick frozen (IQF). Products are quick frozen and individually layered in the case. Typical packing procedure for things like portion-cut boneless, skinless chicken breasts.

Ineligible bidder. Company that would like to bid for a buyer's business, but would not be allowed to bid because it does not meet certain qualifications set by the buyer. For instance, the company may not be large enough, it may not have sufficient financial strength, and so forth.

Informal specification. Less precise specification. Usually includes only information the vendor uses to describe the product in its catalog.

Ingredient room. Area set aside in the main storeroom where an employee measures out all the ingredients needed for all the recipes to be prepared during the shift, and then issues them to the appropriate kitchen locations.

In-process inventory. Products located at employee work stations; most or all will be used during the shift.

Installation and testing costs. Typical charges paid when making a major equipment purchase. Usually paid in addition to the AP price of the equipment, though a buyer's company may be able to provide these services personally for less.

Institute of Supply Management (ISM). Organization that offers relevant information, education, and training to purchasing professionals.

Institutional can size. A No. 10 can. It holds up to 3 quarts, or from 96 to 105 ounces, of product.

Institutional Meat Purchase Specification (IMPS) number. Numbering system for meat items. For instance, if buyers order a number 1112 ribeye steak, they will consistently receive a very specific type of product, no matter which meat vendor they buy from.

Instructions to bidders. Required process vendors must follow when submitting a competitive bid. Typically also includes a description of how the winning bid will be determined and the qualifications vendors need in order to be allowed to bid.

Intended use. Refers to the performance requirement of a product or service, which is noted on the specification. Considered to be the most important piece of information on a specification.

Interest group. Another term for newsgroup.

Interest on unpaid balance. Finance charge added to the portion of a bill the buyer does not pay immediately. Can be avoided if the entire balance is paid off. Alternately, a fee or penalty for late payment.

Intermediary. Another term for vendor.

International Foodservice Manufacturers Association (IFMA). Organization whose primary membership is employed in the foodservice equipment trade. Provides relevant information and professional development opportunities to its members. Also helps ensure that their interests are represented in the marketplace.

Interstate Certified Shellfish Shippers List. Agency within the Food and Drug Administration (FDA) that approves the areas where shellfish are grown and harvested. When a buyer purchases these shellfish, the container will include a tag (that must be kept on hand for at least 90 days) that shows the number of the bed of water where the products were grown and harvested.

Introductory discount. Price reduction by vendors to entice buyers to try something new. May also take the form of buy-one, get-one-free.

Inventory book value. The value of inventory that is supposed to be in storage, as recorded on inventory records, such as a bin card. The value is based upon perpetual inventory calculations.

Inventory classification. Arranging inventory in a specific, organized way so that it is easier to monitor its usage.

Inventory control. System of procedures used to ensure that the products you purchase will be used only as intended. The main objective is to make certain that the actual usage is the same, or about the same, as the expected usage.

Inventory padding. Reporting a false inventory amount by indicating that there is more inventory on hand. A fraud that is usually committed in order to make the actual cost of food sold appear to be less than it is.

Inventory sales control. Another term for critical item inventory analysis.

Inventory shrinkage. Another term for pilferage.

Inventory substitution. Occurs when someone takes a product and leaves behind a different one. Typically done by persons who steal a high-quality item and substitute a low-quality one in its place.

Inventory-taking service. An outside contractor who comes to your restaurant to take a physical inventory of the products you have at your restaurant. In addition, the contractor may perform related duties, such as valuing the inventory and preparing purchase orders.

Inventory turnover. Equal to the actual cost of food used (or sold) divided by the average inventory value kept at the restaurant.

Invoice. A bill from a vendor for goods or services, often presented as the goods are delivered or after the services are performed.

Invoice padding. Adding extra charges and/or items to the invoice that were not ordered. This could happen because of an innocent mistake, or it could be done by someone trying to steal from your restaurant.

Invoice receiving. Common type of receiving procedure. Involves comparing the invoice with the order record, and then proceeding to check quality, quantity, and AP prices of the items delivered.

Invoice scam. Using fraudulent invoices to steal from a company.

Invoice stamp. Information placed on the receiving agent's copy of the invoice that indicates all appropriate checks were made and that the shipment was accepted.

Invoices on account. Bill-paying method. Involves reconciling all invoices and credit slips received during the billing period with the end-of-period statement sent by the vendor. If everything is correct, the company pays the total amount listed on the end-of-period statement, or makes the minimum payment and lets the balance ride until the next period.

Issuing procedure. There are two types: formal and informal. The formal procedure requires a product user, such as a chef, to requisition products from a central warehouse or storage facility. The chef signs for the items and is responsible for them. An informal procedure allows the product user to request from the manager what is needed, with the manager getting the products and handling the paperwork later on. Another informal process allows any product user to enter the warehouse or storage facility and take what's needed for production and/or service.

Itemized bill. Invoice that indicates each item's AP price and extended price, as well as all other costs, such as delivery charges, associated with the purchase.

Jug wine. Refers to a product typically served as the house wine. Usually packed in large containers, such as bag-in-the-box containers.

Just-in-time inventory management. A system that attempts to ensure that the moment the inventory level of a particular product reaches zero, a shipment of that item arrives at your back door. The main objective is to reduce carrying charges to their lowest possible level.

Kickback. An illegal gift given by a vendor to someone if he or she will agree to help defraud the restaurant. An illegal rebate.

Kitchen steward. Person who supervises the warewashing and cleaning staff. May also have some purchasing responsibilities.

Landed cost. The cost used by the vendor in a cost-plus buying arrangement.

Layered packaging. Products packed between sheets of paper, plastic, or cardboard. Intended to protect them so that they do not break or otherwise lose quality.

Layout pack. Products are packed in layers that can be lifted from the case and placed in other containers for storage or production. For example, layout sliced bacon may be layered on baking sheets that can be placed on sheet pans and cooked off in the oven.

Lead time. Period of time between when you place an order with a vendor and when you receive it.

Leasing company. Firm that purchases FFE and leases them to other companies. The typical rental plan is a rent-to-own arrangement. May be a more expensive form of financing a FFE purchase than borrowing the money and buying the items outright.

License state. A state that grants licenses to importers-wholesalers, distributors, and retailers who together handle the distribution and sale of beverage alcohol.

Lien-sale contract. Allows the service provider, usually some type of construction, decorating, or designer service, to attach a lien to the entire property if he or she is not paid for the work performed.

Lifetime cost. A term typically used when analyzing an equipment purchase. Along with the AP price of the item, the buyer might also examine the trade-in value of the old equipment, the cost of the energy needed to operate the equipment, extra charges for delivery, set-up, and training, how much it can sell for when it is time to replace it, and so forth.

Limited purchase order (LPO). A purchase order that restricts how much a buyer can purchase. There are limits on the quantity that can be purchased and/or the amount of money that can be spent at one time.

Line-item purchasing. A practice of buying from vendors only the individual items on a competitive bid sheet that are priced lower than those submitted by competing vendors. For instance, if a purveyor bids on 10 items, but is the lowest bidder on only 1 of them, the buyer will buy only the 1 item. Sometimes referred to as *cherry picking*. The opposite of bottom-line, firm-price purchasing.

Liquidation. Selling off business assets in order to satisfy creditors. May be done via auction.

Liquor distributor. Another term for vendor. Purchases beverage alcohol from primary sources and resells it to retailers.

Liquor license. Granted by a government agency. Gives the licensee the authority to purchase and sell beverage alcohol.

LISTSERV. Electronic mailing list that sends messages automatically to all members.

Logistics software. Computer program used by vendors to outline the routing sequences its delivery drivers must follow when delivering shipments. Intended to increase delivery efficiency.

Long-term contract. Agreement that typically lasts at least one year.

Loss leader. Product sold at a much lower profit margin in order to attract customers who will purchase it, as well as other more profitable items.

Lost leader. Product sold at a negative profit margin in order to attract customers who will purchase it, as well as other more profitable items.

Lot number. An indication that packaged goods originated from a particular group, or lot. Important if, for example, you are purchasing canned goods; products coming from the same batch will have similar culinary quality whereas those from different lots may be slightly different.

Lowball bid. A competitive bid that is artificially low. Vendors may lowball a buyer, hoping to get their foot in the door; later on, they will try to hike the AP price substantially.

Lug. Container that has two layers of product. Term typically used in the fresh produce trade.

Mailing list. Similar to a newsgroup. Uses e-mail to send messages to groups of individuals who have the same interests. Alternately, a group of snail mail addresses that receive information, such as product promotions and sales solicitations, through the U.S. Postal Service.

Maintenance contract. Type of extended warranty coverage. For a fee, usually paid monthly, the contractor provides routine maintenance as well as emergency service. Typically purchased when the initial warranty period is set to expire.

Make-goods. Free advertising time or space granted to buyers when the actual intended audience size is smaller than the guaranteed one.

Make-or-buy analysis. A cost/benefit analysis whereby the buyer tries to determine if it is more economical to purchase raw foods and make the finished product in-house, or whether it may be less expensive to purchase a convenience food. The buyer usually considers the cost of food, labor, overhead, labor skill available, and so on when making the decision.

Manual list. A moderated electronic mailing list. Unless messages are approved by the moderator, they will not be sent to group members.

Manufacturer's agent. Similar to a manufacturer's representative, but not the same. Main difference is that the agent typically works for only one primary source, whereas the manufacturer's representative typically works for several.

Manufacturer's representative. Similar to a broker, but not the same; main difference is that the rep will typically provide end-user services, whereas the broker will not. Also similar to a manufacturer's agent, but not the same; main difference is that the agent typically works for only one primary source, whereas the manufacturer's representative typically works for several.

Manufacturing grade. A very low grade given to food products that are not intended to be sold as fresh items, but are meant to be used by manufacturers to produce a finished item. For example, low-grade beef usually is purchased by a manufacturer that makes things like canned chili or canned beef stew.

Marinade pack. A packing medium intended to impart flavor, and sometimes tenderness, to foods. For instance, if you feature spicy wings on your menu, you may decide to purchase fresh wings marinated in a special sauce. When they arrive at your restaurant they are ready to cook; you do not need to marinate them yourself.

Marketing board. Web site dedicated to selling a specific product or group of products.

Marketing terms for fish. Names used by members of the fish channel of distribution to identify various types and forms of fish products. Alternately, names used by seafood marketers to make their fish products seem more attractive, which typically involves changing the current name of a product in order to make it more salable.

Market quote buying. Another term for call sheet buying.

Materials budget. Involves setting a dollar limit of how much a buyer is able to purchase over a particular time period. A method used to control and evaluate a buyer's performance.

Meat Buyers Guide (MBG) number. Another term for Institutional Meat Purchase Specification (IMPS) number.

Meat Buyers Guide, The. Publication that standardizes, organizes and identifies various types and cuts of meat products. A numbering system is used for easy reference.

Meat tag. Used to control the usage of expensive items, such as meat, fish, and poultry. It contains two duplicate parts. One part is attached to the item when it is received and placed into storage, the other one goes to the controller's office. When an item is taken from storage and issued to production, the part on the item is removed and sent to the controller, who matches it with the other part. The item is then removed from the inventory file. At that point, the storage supervisor (storeroom manager) is no longer responsible for the item, the chef is.

Media-buying service. A type of advertising agency that helps clients develop their overall advertising strategies and selects the various media to use. Works for commissions.

Memo invoice. Another term for goods received without invoice slip.

Menu mix percentage. Indication of a menu item's popularity. Equal to the number of the menu item sold divided by the number of all menu items sold during a defined period of time, multiplied by 100. Usually used to help chefs forecast sales revenue, how much food to buy, how much labor to schedule, and so forth.

Menu price calculation. The food cost of the menu item divided by its food cost percentage.

Merchant wholesaler. Another term for vendor.

Merits. Refers to one way advertising is paid for. The price a buyer pays is directly related to the amount of sales revenue generated by the advertising.

Middleman. Another term for vendor.

Minimal inventory investment. Refers to the buyer's desire to have only enough inventory necessary to conduct business. Intended to minimize carrying costs.

Minimum order requirement. The least amount of an item a buyer needs to purchase before a vendor will agree to sell it. Alternately, the least amount a buyer needs to purchase before he or she can qualify for free delivery.

Minimum weight per case. Important selection factor when purchasing products that may vary in weight from one vendor to another, or because of other factors, such as seasonal variations. Helps ensure that the buyer receives a predictable amount of product

Mixed case. A case that contains more than one type of item. Usually found in the beverage alcohol trade, where the vendor will allow the buyer to purchase a case of 12 bottles, but each bottle may be a different product. Vendors may allow this for products you purchase that you don't sell very quickly, such as specialty bourbons. Vendors who sell mixed cases are usually willing to charge the case price per unit for each item.

Modified atmosphere packaging (MAP). Another term for controlled atmosphere packaging (CAP).

Move list. A list of products that need to be sold ASAP. For instance, they may be on the verge of spoilage, or they might be discontinued items. If vendors have items on a move list they may call you to see if you're interested in any of them. Usually the AP prices of these items are deep discounted.

Muzz-go list. Another term for move list.

National contract. Clause in a contract between a large, multiunit restaurant company and a vendor stipulating that all restaurants in the chain will receive the same types of products, usually at the same AP prices.

National distribution. Clause in a national contract stipulating that all restaurants in the chain will be able to rely on getting the same types of products delivered to their back doors.

National Restaurant Association (NRA). Trade organization that represents, educates, and promotes the U.S. foodservice industry and the people working in it.

National Restaurant Association Educational Foundation (NRAEF). Agency of the National Restaurant Association (NRA) that provides educational resources, materials, and programs that address recruitment, development, and retention of the industry's workforce. It is dedicated to fulfilling the NRA's educational mission.

National Sanitation Foundation (NSF) International. Provides sanitation certification for FFE items that meet its standards.

Negative selling. Occurs when a vendor places the buyer in a position where the buyer encourages the vendor to take the buyer's order (and money). Usually done by convincing the buyer that he or she must use that particular vendor and that there is no substitute vendor capable of handling the order. More likely to occur when purchasing consulting services than when purchasing any other type of product or service.

Negotiation. To come to terms or to reach an agreement through discussion and a willingness to compromise.

Net weight. Gross weight less the tare weight.

New pack time. Time of the year when products intended for sale the following year (or other period of time) are packed. For instance, canned fruits and vegetables are usually processed and packed right after harvest. Vendors then work off of this inventory until the next new pack time rolls around.

New vs. used FFE. Major selection factor when purchasing FFE. Although used products may be cheaper, they may lack the benefits of newer items. And they may not last as long as new ones.

Newsgroup. An electronic bulletin board where many individuals who have a common interest can post messages.

Night delivery. Shipment delivered during off-hours. Intended to save money because there is less traffic for the driver to contend with, which means that more deliveries can be made.

Night drop. When the delivery driver has a key to the facility, enters it when closed for business, leaves the shipment, locks up, and goes. The hospitality operator puts the shipment away when he or she comes in the next morning. Intended to reduce costs due to the efficiency of deliveries at off hours (i.e., late-night or early-morning) and not having to pay a receiving agent.

Nitrogen flush. A gas-flushed pack. Using nitrogen in order to remove air, thereby removing all oxygen from the package. Done to enhance shelf life.

No-name brand. Another term for generic brand.

North American Association of Food Equip. Mfrs. (NAFEM). Trade organization representing companies in Canada, the United States, and Mexico that manufacture commercial foodservice equipment and supplies.

North American Meat Processors Association (NAMP). Trade organization representing meat processing companies and associates who share a continuing commitment to provide their customers with safe, reliable, and consistent meat, poultry, seafood, game, and other related products.

Number of pieces per bird. Selection factor that may be important when purchasing poultry. Refers directly to the number of parts to be cut from a bird carcass, and indirectly to the style of cut that will be used.

Odd-hours discount. Price break awarded to buyers who allow vendors to deliver shipments at unusual times, such as late at night when the restaurant is closed, or during the sacred hours.

One-stop shopping. Buying as much as you can from one purveyor, or the fewest possible purveyors.

Online auction site. Electronic auction, allowing prospective buyers to bid on products without being physically present. Usually all details are handled over the Internet.

Online ordering system. Ordering products from vendors over the Internet or directly from a purveyor using his or her proprietary software.

Opening inventory. Another term for beginning inventory.

Open market buying. Another term for call sheet buying.

Open storeroom. An unlocked storage facility that can be accessed by employees as needed. Usually contains the less-expensive foods, beverages, and nonfood supplies.

Opportunity buy. A purchase intended to save a great deal of money. The products are price discounted. A quantity discount is an example of an opportunity buy.

Opportunity cost. By choosing to do something, you give up the option of doing something else. For instance, if you pay a bill too early you lose the option of investing the money and earning some interest income. The loss of income in this case is considered to be the opportunity cost.

Ordering cost. The amount of money spent to make an order, receive it, and store it. Includes things such as labor needed to perform the work and administrative costs, such as faxing, photocopying, and cell phone charges.

Ordering procedures. Standardized process used by the buyer to ensure that the correct amounts of needed products are ordered at the appropriate time.

Order modifier. Software in a computerized point-of-sale (POS) system that forces the server to answer questions about a guest's order. For instance, if the server enters a steak into the system, the computer will ask, "What temperature?" The server will then answer the question to complete the order before sending it to the kitchen printer.

Organic food. Natural food grown, produced, packaged, and delivered without the use of synthetic chemicals and fertilizers. Primary sources and distributors must adhere to the organic guidelines and standards published by the USDA.

Outsourcing. Identifying work that is not central to your restaurant company's primary mission and hiring an outside service to do it for you instead of doing it yourself. Things such as pest control and gardening services are usually outsourced.

Overrun. The amount of air whipped into a frozen product.

Packed under continuous government inspection. Selection factor some buyers may specify when purchasing food products (such as fresh produce and fish) that are not legally required to be produced under continuous government inspection.

Packed Under Federal Inspection (PUFI). Seal placed on the product labels of fish items that have been produced and packed under continuous government inspection by the U.S. Department of Commerce (USDC).

Packers' brand name. Very specific indication of product quality. More precise than a brand name. A packer's personal grading system. Usually intended to take the place of U.S. quality grades.

Packer's grade. Another term for packer's brand.

Packing date. Date that a product was packaged. May be written in code or in plain language.

Packing medium. The type of liquid used to pack foods. Especially relevant when purchasing canned goods.

Packing slip. Another term for invoice. Typically accompanies a shipment delivered by a common carrier.

Paid-out. Refers to taking money out of the cash drawer and using it to pay a bill. For example, if you run low on ice, you could take money out of the cash drawer, give it to an employee, and ask him or her to run down to the supermarket to buy some bagged ice. When the employee returns, the bill for the bagged ice is placed in the cash drawer so that the missing cash can be accounted for at the end of the shift.

Panic buying. Occurs when a buyer is in a pinch and will pay any price to get the stuff right now.

Par stock. The maximum amount of a product you want to have on-hand. When reordering the product you want to buy just enough to bring you up to par.

Payment terms. Another name for credit terms.

Perpetual inventory. Keeping a running balance of an inventory item so that you always know what you have on hand. When a shipment is received you add to the balance and every time you use some of it you deduct that amount. Similar to keeping an up-to-date cash balance in your personal checkbook.

Personal purchase. Another term for steward sale.

Personalized packaging. Unique packaging produced according to the buyer's specific requirements. Normally includes the buyer's company logo and/or other proprietary marks.

Physical inventory. An actual counting and valuing of all products kept in your restaurant.

Pick-up memo. Gives the driver permission to pick up something from you. Typically used when you want to return a product to the vendor and you arrange to have it picked up when the driver makes the next regularly scheduled delivery of things you purchased. May also be used when a driver is delivering a substitute piece of equipment (such as a coffee urn) and needs to pick up the one you have so that it can be taken back to the shop for repair.

Pilferage. Refers to minor theft. For instance, employees snatching a drink while on the clock, or guests swiping an ash tray.

Plant visit. Refers to a buyer making a personal visit to a vendor's facilities to evaluate its product line and its production and distribution systems.

Point of origin. Refers to the part of the world where a product originates. Important selection factor for some food items, as the point of origin can have a significant impact on their culinary quality.

Point-of-Sale (POS) system. Computerized retail sales system that streamlines ordering and order processing and maintains a considerable amount of information, such as guest counts, server productivity statistics, types of payments, and so forth.

Popularity index. Another term for menu mix percentage.

Portability. Refers to the ability of an item to be easily and inexpensively moved to, and operated in, various locations. Important selection factor for FFE.

Portion cut. Equal to one serving. Typically refers to precut steaks and chops that are all the same weight.

Post-off. Term used for a discount offered by a beverage alcohol vendor.

Postmix. Refers to a nonalcoholic beverage concentrate, such as frozen juice concentrate or soda pop syrup, that must be reconstituted just before serving it to customers.

Potential supplier. Vendor that a buyer feels should be evaluated in order to determine if he or she should be added to the approved-supplier list.

Precious room. Locked area inside an open storeroom or walk-in refrigerator (or freezer). Typically contains high-priced merchandise. For instance, a walk-in refrigerator may contain a locked cage that contains all the expensive steaks that can be accessed only by the chef and/or the manager on duty.

Precut. Another term for portion cut.

Precut fresh produce. Refers to fresh produce that has been chopped or otherwise cut, and packaged in cello wrap or other similar type of packaging material.

Preferred-provider procurement. Another term for one-stop shopping.

Premium brand. Indicates that the product is high quality and usually high priced.

Premium well brand. A well brand that is higher quality than the typical well brand poured by most bars.

Premix. Refers to a ready-to-serve nonalcoholic beverage, such as a 12-ounce can of Coke.

Prepaid order. Another term for purchase order draft system.

Price club. Another term for buying club.

Price control. Refers to government agencies dictating the minimum price that must be charged for a product. This type of control is fairly common in the dairy and beverage alcohol distribution channels.

Price extension. Another term for extended price.

Price limitation. Another term for cost limitation.

Price maintenance. Another term for price control.

Primal cut. Another term for wholesale cut.

Primary source. A supplier at the beginning of a product's channel of distribution. For instance, a farmer is a primary source for fresh produce items. This supplier typically sells items to an intermediary that resells them to the restaurant community.

Prime-vendor account. A consistent and significantly large account a buyer has with a vendor that, because of its size and the loyalty of the buyer, may be eligible for discounts and/or other special privileges. Alternately, another term for house account.

Prime-vendor discount. Price reduction if you purchase most of your products from a single vendor. You may have to buy as much as 90 percent of your total purchases in order to qualify for a discount.

Prime-vendor procurement. Another term for one-stop shopping.

Procurement. An orderly, systematic exchange between a seller and a buyer. The process of obtaining goods and services, including all activities associated with determining the types of products needed, making purchases, receiving and storing shipments, and administering purchase contracts.

Produce Marketing Association (PMA). Trade association representing members who market fresh fruits, vegetables, and related products worldwide. Its members are involved in the production, distribution, retail, and foodservice sectors of the industry.

Product analysis. Evaluating various products in order to determine which one represents the best value. Alternately, another term for critical item inventory analysis.

Product compatibility. The extent to which a product is able to interact well with other products. A typical example would be purchasing a new piece of equipment because it would fit nicely with the current equipment.

Product cost percentage. Equal to cost of a product divided by its selling price, multiplied by 100. A typical example would be the food cost percentage.

Product effectiveness. The extent to which a product lives up to its vendor's claims. A typical example would be the ability of an all-purpose cleaner to clean satisfactorily any type of surface.

Product form. Refers to the degree of processing, or lack thereof, a product has when you purchase it. For instance, a buyer can purchase whole chickens or just the chicken parts he or she wants. The parts typically would cost more than the whole birds.

Product identification. Another term for specification.

Product odor. Refers to the scent some products, such as cleaning solutions, may have. Alternately, a factor considered when checking product freshness.

Product preservation. Refers to production, storage, and/or delivery procedures a vendor uses to ensure consistent and reliable product quality. Alternately, process used to increase an item's shelf life.

Product safety. Refers to the level of risk incurred when using some products, such as cleaning solutions.

Product size. Refers to the buyer's specified weight, or volume, of a particular item he or she wants to purchase. Examples would be a 10-ounce steak or a 4-ounce hamburger.

Product status. Indicates whether a product is available from the vendor or if it is back-ordered.

Product specification. Another term for specification.

Product's performance requirement. Another term for intended use.

Product substitution. Item delivered by a vendor that is not what was originally ordered, but is an acceptable substitute. Alternately, use of a different, but acceptable, product in a standardized recipe.

Product testing. Refers to the process a buyer will use to evaluate a product before purchasing it. Alternately, refers to the process a receiving agent will use to evaluate a product before agreeing to accept it from the delivery driver.

Production loss. The difference between the AP weight and the EP weight.

Profit markup. The difference between the vendor's cost of a product and its sales price. Alternately, the difference between the EP cost of a menu item and its menu price.

Promotional discount. The AP price is discounted if the buyer allows the vendor to promote the product in the restaurant. Or if the restaurant operator agrees to personally help promote the sale of the product to his or her customers.

Propertary pass. A document the employee must obtain from the chef or another manager and show to security in order to remove items from the restaurant.

Proprietary brand. Another term for packers' brand name.

Proprietary-brand discount. A price reduction if you purchase a large amount of products that carry the vendor's proprietary brand name.

Pull date. The date at which a product should not be used, or should not be sold.

Pulp temperature. Internal temperature of precut, convenience fresh produce products, such as chopped salad greens.

Purchase order. A request that the vendor deliver what you want, ideally at the time you want it, at an agreed-upon AP price and credit terms. May include other conditions, such as minimum order amount, cost of delivery (if any), and so forth.

Purchase order draft system. A purchase order that includes an attached check to cover the price of the goods and/or services. A form of prepaid order.

Purchase requisition. Lists the products or services needed by someone in the restaurant operation. It is given to the buyer, who then goes into the marketplace to find the best deals. This requisition is typically used for things that the buyer doesn't purchase on a regular basis.

Purchasing. Paying for a product or service.

Purchasing policy. Standard procedure that buyer must adhere to when performing his or her duties.

Purchasing power. Refers to the amount of money a buyer spends purchasing products and services. The more money spent, the more ability he or she has to get better deals from vendors.

Purveyor. Another term for vendor.

Quality assurance. Another term for quality control.

Quality control. Systems and procedures used by managers to ensure that the actual quality of finished items is consistent with the expected quality.

Quality standard. The type of quality you consistently use and that the restaurant is known for. Buyers typically communicate this standard to vendors by specifying brand names and government grades.

Quantity discount. A reward for buying a large amount of one specific type of merchandise.

Quantity limitation. Constraint that indicates the maximum amount of a product or service a buyer can purchase at any one time.

Ready-to-serve product. Convenience food that can be served right out of the container, with no additional preparation other than perhaps thawing and/or reheating.

Ready-to-use product. Convenience food that requires a little bit of preparation in the restaurant's kitchen in order to make it ready for service. For example, cleaned, chopped salad greens will still need to be combined with other ingredients, such as tomatoes and salad dressing, before it can be served to guests.

Rebate. Another term for cash rebate.

Reciprocal buying. "You buy from me, I'll buy from you."

Reconciling the vendor's end-of-period statement. See invoices on account.

Reconditioned FFE. FFE that have undergone major remodeling and/or retrofitting. Usually done because it may be less expensive than purchasing new FFE.

Recycling. Refers to taking a used product and/or its parts and reusing them after they have undergone a reconditioning process. Alternately, taking a used product and/or its parts and creating something new and different that can be used for another purpose.

Reference book. Information that is computerized or made available in hard copy, for the purpose of researching product characteristics needed to prepare specifications.

Reference check. Confirming the veracity of information and personal accomplishments provided by vendors and job candidates.

Referral group. A type of co-op where independent operators join together in order to send business to each other. For instance, Best Western is a lodging referral group that has a central reservations system available to each member. In addition, these groups typically provide some purchasing advantages, as well as other types of support, to its members.

Relationship marketing. Procedure that does not view marketing as selling products one-at-a-time—that is, it does not view marketing as a series of individual transactions. Instead, it refers to the need for vendors and customers to form personal alliances that will lead to the sale and purchase of products and services that mutually benefit each other.

Rent-to-own plan. See leasing company.

Reorder point (ROP). The lowest amount of stock on hand that you feel comfortable with, the point that you will not go below before ordering more stock.

Request for bid. Another term for request for quote (RFQ).

Request for credit memo. Another term for credit memo.

Request for quote (RFQ). Used by buyers who shop around for the best possible deals. It is a list of items needed and their specifications, given to potential vendors who are then asked to quote, or bid, the AP prices they would charge for them.

Requisition. Another term for purchase requisition. Alternately, another term for stock requisition.

Responsible bidder. Opposite of ineligible bidder. Company that is considered large enough, has sufficient financial strength, has a good reputation and history of satisfactory performance, and so forth, and because of this, is placed on a buyer's approved-supplier list.

Restocking fee. Fee the vendor charges the buyer who wants to return something that isn't defective, but that he or she just found out can't be used, or if the buyer wants to return special-order merchandise. Typically occurs when the buyer changes his or her mind at the last minute and tries to send the shipment back to the vendor.

Returns policy. Vendor's procedure a buyer needs to follow in order to return products and receive credit for them.

Reverse auction. Process whereby a buyer makes it known that he or she wants to purchase something and asks sellers to bid for his or her business. Instead of buyers bidding for a seller's products, sellers bid for a buyer's purchase order. Typically conducted online.

RFID tags. Radio Frequency Identification tags placed on boxes, crates, pallets, etc. They are used by distributors and retailers to monitor automatically, inventory and storage areas. A wireless technology is used—the same technology that allows electronic wireless toll payment in many states or the ExxonMobil Speed-Pass wireless payment system—to transmit data wirelessly to a sensor. It could be argued that RFID tags are a major improvement over the bar code technology used by most distributors and retailers today.

Ripening process used. Can be natural or artificial ripening. Important selection factor when purchasing some fresh produce products.

Ripening room. Closed storage area used to ripen some fresh produce products, such as bananas. The storage area is sealed and ethylene gas is introduced in order to induce and hasten the ripening process.

Risk-purchasing group. A co-op that specializes in the purchase of insurance for its members.

Route salesperson. The driver who delivers standing orders to the restaurant.

Sacred hours. Time of the day when you would not want to accept deliveries. Usually these hours are from 11:30 a.m. to 1:30 p.m.

Safety stock. Extra stock kept on hand to avoid running out and disappointing the guest.

Sales rep. Another term for distributor sales rep (DSR).

Sales tax. Tax a company must pay to state and local governments for things purchased, such as cleaning chemicals, that will not be resold to customers.

Salvage buy. Buying a deep-discounted item. Usually the AP price is very low because the item is damaged.

Sample. Testing a small portion of a product or a shipment in order to determine its overall quality and acceptability. Alternately, see free sample.

Sealed bid. Typically done with fixed bid buying. The AP price quotations are secret until they are all opened at once.

Search engine. Refers to a program used to crawl the Internet in order to locate Web sites and other materials related to specific key words entered by the user.

Security agreement. Contract used to secure a loan. If the borrower fails to pay, it allows the lender to foreclose and take the asset(s) used to collateralize the loan.

Selection. Choosing from among various alternatives.

Sell-by date. Another term for pull date.

Seller co-op. Refers to sellers, usually primary sources, who are legally allowed to join together to market their products. Typically found in the fresh produce trade.

Servable cost. Another term for edible-portion (EP) cost.

Servable weight. Another term for edible-portion weight.

Servable yield. Another term for edible yield.

Server. Central computer to which other computers, such as individual personal computers (PCs), are networked. It communicates with all the other computers on the network. Alternately, a person who takes guests' orders for food and beverages and delivers them to the guests.

Service agreement. Covers the cost of FFE defects and malfunctions during the initial warranty period provided by the FFE vendor.

Service contract. Another term for service agreement.

Shared buying. Another term for co-op buying.

Shatter pack. Another term for individually quick frozen (IQF).

Shelf life. The amount of time a product can remain in storage before it loses quality and cannot be used.

Shelf-stable product. A food item that is processed and packaged in such a way that it can maintain its quality at room temperature.

Shingle pack. Layering product in such a way that the pieces overlap and do not completely cover each other. May be done for things like sliced bacon.

Shopping around. Another term for bid buying.

Show-special price. Another term for trade-show discount.

Shrink allowance. The amount of weight loss the buyer will accept in a shipment. The weight loss is due to unavoidable moisture loss during transit.

Shrink wrap. Product is packed in plastic and a vacuum is pulled through it so that air is removed and the wrapping collapses to fit snugly around the product. A type of controlled atmosphere packaging (CAP).

Signature item. A menu item that is very popular; the restaurant is known for it.

Single-source procurement. Another term for one-stop shopping.

Skimming. Another term for pilferage.

Slab-packed. Refers to items tossed into a container in no particular order or style. An inexpensive packing procedure, though it can cause breakage and other quality deterioration for some products.

Slacked out. A food item that is thought to be fresh, but has actually been frozen, thawed, and passed off as fresh. Buyers are most likely to see these types of products when buying fresh fish.

Small stop. Term used by vendors to refer to a hospitality operation that does not purchase very much.

Small wares. Kitchen, dining room, and bar utensils, such as pots, pans, mixing bowls, tableware, and so forth.

Smoking. Product preservation method that removes moisture from food. It also concentrates the food's natural flavor as well as imparting a smoky taste.

Snap pack. Another term for individually quick frozen (IQF). When you remove a layer of frozen items from a case and drop it onto a counter, the IQF portions should snap apart easily. If they do not come apart easily and cleanly, it usually means that they have been thawed a bit and refrozen.

Socially responsible firm. Vendor who uses environmentally safe products and/or procedures. Alternately, vendor who promotes social causes, supports charities, and so forth.

Sole-source procurement. Another term for one-stop shopping.

Solid pack. Packing product in a container with no added juice or water.

Sourcing. The process used by a hospitality company to help establish a supplier. Typically done by large hospitality companies to help establish minority-owned primary sources and/or intermediaries. Alternately, the process a buyer undertakes to locate a vendor for a product or service that is very hard to find.

Specification. A description of all the characteristics in a product required to fill certain production and/or service needs. *Spec,* for short.

Standard cost. The expected cost. Sometimes referred to as the potential cost, the planned cost, the budgeted cost, or the theoretical cost. Typically used to help set menu prices. Also used to compare to the actual cost incurred to determine if management is achieving its budgetary goals.

Standard of fill. A U.S. government regulation that indicates to the manufacturer how full a container must be to avoid deception. It prevents the selling of excessive amounts of air or water in place of food.

Standard of identity. A U.S. government regulation that essentially establishes what a food product is in order to carry a certain name. For example, what a food product must be in order to be labeled "strawberry preserves."

Standard of quality. A U.S. government regulation that states the minimum quality a product must meet in order to earn the federal government's lowest possible quality grade. Products below the minimum quality standard must indicate on the package label what the problem is. For instance, if canned green beans are excessively broken, the label could read, "below standard of quality: excessively broken."

Standard recipe. A set of precise procedures used to produce a food or beverage menu item. Includes such things as a list of ingredients, the amount of each ingredient, preparation methods, and so forth.

Standard yield. The yield expected if everything works out according to plan. Results when an item is produced according to established standard production procedures outlined in the standard recipe. For example, if the standard specifications are followed for a meat item and it is then properly trimmed, cooked, and portioned, the actual yield should closely approximate the standard yield.

Standing order. Under this procedure, a driver (usually referred to as a route salesperson) shows up, takes inventory of what you have, then takes off the truck enough product to bring you up to some predetermined par stock, enough to last until he or she visits you the next time. The driver writes up a delivery ticket after it's determined what you need.

State grade. A quality grade given by a state agency, which could be used on the specification in lieu of a U.S. quality grade or brand name identification. For instance, Wisconsin has a state grading system for cheese.

Steam table pack. Convenience food items packed in a container that can be popped into an oven or combi-steamer to reheat the food inside. When hot, the top of the container is removed and the container is then placed directly into a steam table or chaffing dish and kept warm for service. The typical container is usually made out of aluminum.

Steward. Manager who has food-buying responsibilities. May also be responsible for the food storage areas.

Steward sale. A sale of your inventory to employees. You charge them the price you paid. In effect, you allow them to take advantage of your purchasing power for their personal benefit.

Stockless purchasing. When a buyer purchases a large amount of product (for example, a three-month supply) and arranges for the vendor to store it and deliver a little at a time.

Stockout. Running out of a product; not having it available for guests who want it.

Stockout cost. The cost incurred when you do not have a product a guests wants. Although the cost cannot always be calculated, in the long run there will usually be a negative impact on your bottom line. For example, the guest leaves without buying anything. Or the guest stays and orders something else, but never comes back.

Stock requisition. A formal request made by an employee for items needed to carry out necessary tasks. It is given to the person managing the storage facilities. A typical control document used by large hotels.

Stock rotation. A system of using older products first. When a shipment arrives, the older stock is moved to the front of the shelf and the newer stock is placed behind it.

Storage cost. Another term for carrying cost.

Storefront dealer. FFE company that carries a minimum amount of inventory. Usually specializes in handling small, portable types of FFE.

Sun-dried. Product with a moisture content of approximately 25 percent.

Supplier. Another term for vendor. Alternately, a very large primary source that manufactures and/or processes products that are then sold through intermediaries.

Supplier selection criteria. Characteristics a buyer considers when determining if potential vendors should be added to the approved-supplier list.

Supplier services. Services, such as free delivery, generous credit terms, etc., provided by vendors to buyers who purchase their products.

Support functions. Another term for supplier services.

Supporting local suppliers. Done in order to maintain good relationships with businesspersons who live and work in the local community.

Systems mentality. Ability to view and understand the entire organization and the multitude of relationships it contains.

Systems sale. Usually occurs when buying equipment that requires parts made by only one manufacturer, usually the manufacturer that made the equipment in the first place. For example, buying a dish machine that cannot use other companies' dish racks. Over the long run, a systems sale will cost you more money.

Tagged fish. See Interstate Certified Shellfish Shippers List.

Tare weight. Weight of all material, such as cardboard, wrapping paper, and ice, used to pack and ship the product that is not part of the product itself. Subtracted from gross weight in order to compute net weight.

Target cost percentage. The desired standard cost, expressed as a percentage of sales revenue.

Target market. The customer base your restaurant is set up to service.

Theft. Premeditated burglary.

Theoretical food cost. What the total cost of food sold should be if everything goes according to plan. Sometimes referred to as the potential cost, the planned cost, the budgeted cost, or the standard cost. It is calculated by taking the number sold of each menu item, multiplying them by their respective recipe costs, and adding them all up. The actual cost of food sold, though, may be more or less than expected.

Theoretical inventory usage. Expected amount of inventory usage based on recorded sales. For instance, if 100 steaks are recorded as sold, there should be only 100 steaks missing from inventory.

Theoretical inventory value. What the inventory value is supposed to be based on what you sold. For instance, if you had 100 steaks in inventory worth $5 apiece and the POS system says you sold 50, then there should be $250 worth of steaks left (50 × $5).

An actual count, though, may reveal that you have more or less than $250.

Theoretical sales revenue. What the sales revenue should be based on how much inventory you used. For instance, if you used 100 large soda pop Dixie cups that sell for $2.75 apiece, the POS system should indicate that 100 large soda pops were sold. There should also be $275.00 (100 × $2.75) in the cash drawer.

Third-party dot-com company. Firm that develops software packages, such as e-procurement applications.

Thomas Food and Beverage Market Place. A searchable online or CD database buyers can use to locate vendors, product categories, and individual products.

Tied-house laws. Legislation that prohibits liquor distributors from becoming liquor primary sources or liquor retailers.

Time- and temperature-sensitive food labels. Labels that typically change color when the product is too old and/or when the product has been too long in the danger zone.

Time efficiency program. Software used by vendors to estimate driver downtime and the amount of product that should be delivered per hour by taking into account street traffic flow, various times of the day, and the expected time spent loading and unloading shipments.

Toner-phoner. Term used to identify a scam artist who contacts people and misleads them into purchasing some junk for a high price. A typical scam is to call and offer to sell printer toner for a bargain basement price, hence the term toner-phoner.

Trade association. Organization of people and/or companies who have a common purpose and interest.

Trade association standard. Minimum performance standard for items the association members produce.

Trade-in allowance. Amount of money a vendor credits your account when you buy a new piece of FFE (especially equipment) and turn in an older model.

Trade-out. Refers to bartering your goods and services instead of paying cash. This term is commonly used to refer to trades between restaurants and advertising firms.

Trade relations. The practice of spreading your purchase dollars among several vendors. Intended to create positive publicity for your restaurant.

Trade show. Event where vendors display and sell their products. May also include other activities, such as educational offerings, awards banquets, and so forth.

Trade-show discount. A reward for buying something off the trade show floor. Usually need to pay cash for it and take it as-is, where-is. In the case of equipment, there may not be a guarantee, or if there is, it may be much shorter than the typical one offered if you bought a brand new item.

Transfer slip. Document used to control and account for products moved from one unit to another one within the same company. For instance, if you run a Red Lobster and you send food product over to another Red Lobster on the other side of town because it's running low, the transfer slip will credit your food cost while debiting the other unit's food cost.

Trim. Another term for waste.

Tying agreement. Illegal contract that forces a buyer to purchase from a vendor certain items he or she may not want in order to gain the privilege of purchasing other items the buyer does want.

Ultra-high temperature (UHT). See ultra-pasteurized (UP).

Ultra-pasteurized (UP). Pasteurization process using ultra-high temperatures (UHT). Used to produce a shelf-stable product, such as cream, that is packed in aseptic packages.

Unconditional lien release. Document verifying that a vendor has been paid in full. Typically used in the construction trades to protect a buyer who has signed a lien-sale contract. Once the vendor signs it, he or she is prevented from placing a lien on the property.

Underwriters Laboratories (UL). Provides electrical safety certification for electrical powered equipment that meet its standards.

Uniform Commercial Code (UCC). Legislation outlining rules and regulations pertaining to various business transactions, such as leases, contracts, bills of lading, and so forth. Ensures consistency throughout the United States.

United Fresh Fruit & Vegetable Association. Trade organization that helps promote the growth and success of produce companies and their partners in the channel of distribution. Represents the interests of growers, shippers, processors, brokers, wholesalers, and distributors of produce.

United States Department of Agriculture (USDA). Among other responsibilities, it has inspection powers throughout the food distribution channel. Typically concentrates its inspection efforts on red meat, poultry, and egg production.

United States Department of Commerce (USDC). Agency that, among other things, will, for a fee, provide to seafood processors continuous government inspection and federal grading of their fish products.

Universal Product Code (UPC). Another term for bar code.

Usable cost. Another term for edible-portion (EP) cost.

Usable yield. Another term for yield.

Usable weight. Another term for edible-portion weight.

Used merchandise. Second-hand items, especially second-hand FFE. They are typically purchased in an as-is, where-is condition. Their AP prices are usually much less than comparable new FFE.

Usenet. Refers to a system on the Internet that provides access to several different newsgroups. The newsgroups are typically organized by topic.

User discount. Typical arrangement with vending companies that place machines in your operation. As part of your compensation, you are allowed to use the machines at no-cost, or at a reduced-cost.

Use tax. Tax charged by the state where the buyer's restaurant operation is located (i.e., home state), on products purchased from out-of-state. Similar to the sales tax charged by the home state. Charged by the home state in order to prevent companies from going elsewhere to avoid paying sales tax to their home states.

U.S. procurement grades. Quality grades for poultry. There are two grades: I and II. Unlike other quality grades, these grades are based on the poultry's edible yield; appearance of the birds is deemphasized.

U.S. quality grades. Rating system used by the federal government to indicate the quality of food products. Not all foods have established federal government quality grading standards.

U.S. yield grades. Rating system used by the federal government to indicate the yield of meat products. Not all meats have established federal government yield grading standards.

Value-added food. Another term for convenience food.

Value-added product. Another term for convenience food. Alternately, it could also refer to a nonfood item that has many upgraded features, such as a kitchen ventilation system that is self-cleaning, as opposed to one that has to be cleaned by hand.

Value analysis. Involves examining a product in order to identify unnecessary costs that can be eliminated without sacrificing over-all quality or performance.

Variance. Difference between what is expected and what actually happened. Typically used to refer to the difference between the standard cost and the actual cost.

Variety meat. Refers to meat, such as liver, kidney, and so forth.

Vendor. A company, usually local, that sells products and services to the restaurant community. It typically purchases the goods it sells from a primary source.

Vendor A list. Refers to a vendor's special group of customers who deserve preferential treatment.

Versatility. An important FFE selection factor. Refers to the ability of an item, such as a toaster oven, to do more than one job.

Vintage. Refers to the year of production. Important selection factor for some wines.

Virtual discussion group. Another term for chat room.

Volume discount. Similar to a quantity discount. The buyer agrees to purchase a huge volume of goods; however, unlike a quantity discount, he or she can buy more than one type of merchandise.

Warehouse club. Another term for wholesale club.

Waste. Unusable part of a product that occurs when it is processed. Most waste is unavoidable, but sometimes avoidable waste occurs due to mistakes and carelessness.

WATS-line hustler. Another term for toner-phoner.

Web-ordering system. Refers to a method of ordering products over the World Wide Web (www). Buyers typically use an e-procurement application to shop around and enter their orders.

Weight range. Indication of the approximate size of a product the buyer wishes to purchase. Used when it is impossible or impractical to specify an exact weight.

Well brand. Refers to the type of drink served to guests when they do not order a specific brand of beverage alcohol.

Wet aging. Shrink wrapping meat, which allows the release of meat enzymes that soften the connective tissues.

Wet-packed. Another term for wet aging.

What-if analysis. Method of analyzing the potential outcome of a particular procedure without actually executing it. Normally involves the use of mathematical models.

Wholesale club. A cash-and-carry operation that is patronized primarily by small restaurants that do not order enough product from vendors to qualify for free delivery. Buyers usually have to pay a membership fee.

Wholesale cut. Refers to a large cut of meat used to produce several retail cuts. It is smaller than a forequarter or hindquarter, but larger than a retail cut.

Wholesaler. Another term for vendor.

Will-call buying. Merchandise is not delivered to the restaurant. The buyer picks it up at the vendor's location. The buyer may also have pay for it when picking it up, unless the buyer's company has established credit with the vendor.

Working storeroom. Refers to a storage area that is kept open during the shift to allow employees to enter as needed in order to retrieve products.

Yield. The net weight or volume of a food item after it has been processed and made ready for sale to the guest.

Yield percentage. The ratio of servable weight to original weight. Equal to servable weight divided by the original weight, multiplied by 100.

Yield test. Process used to determine how much of a purchased product can be served to a guest, how much of it is waste and has to be discarded, and how much of it is edible byproducts that can be used for some other purpose. The result of the test is usually expressed as a yield percentage.

INDEX